Business Sustainability Factors of Performance, Risk, and Disclosure

Business Sustainability Factors of Performance, Risk, and Disclosure

Zabihollah Rezaee

BEP

BUSINESS EXPERT PRESS

Leader in applied, concise business books

Business Sustainability Factors of Performance, Risk, and Disclosure

Copyright © Business Expert Press, LLC, 2021.

Cover design by Charlene Kronstedt

Interior design by Exeter Premedia Services Private Ltd., Chennai, India

First published in 2021 by
Business Expert Press, LLC
222 East 46th Street, New York, NY 10017
www.businessexpertpress.com

ISBN-13: 978-1-63742-006-5 (paperback)
ISBN-13: 978-1-63742-007-2 (e-book)

Business Expert Press Business Law and Corporate Risk Management Collection

Collection ISSN: 2333-6722 (print)
Collection ISSN: 2333-6730 (electronic)

First edition: 2021

10 9 8 7 6 5 4 3 2 1

Description

Business sustainability is advancing from the greenwashing and branding to, very recently, business imperative as shareholders demand, regulators require, and companies report their sustainability performance. Sustainability has become economic and strategic imperative with potential to create opportunities and risks for businesses.

Business Sustainability Factors of Performance, Risk, and Disclosure examines sustainability factors of performance, risk and disclosure. The five dimensions of sustainability performance are economic, governance, social, ethical, and environmental (EGSEE). Sustainability risks are reputational, strategic, operational, compliance, and financial (RSOCF). Sustainability disclosures are relevant to financial economic sustainability performance (ESP) and non-financial environmental, social, and governance (ESG) sustainability performance with ethics are integrated into all other components of sustainability performance.

This book offers guidance for proper measurement, recognition, and reporting of all five EGSEE dimensions of sustainability performance. It also highlights how people, business, and resources collaborate in a business sustainability and accountability model in creating shared value for all stakeholders. The three sustainability factors of performance, risk and disclosure are driven from the stakeholder primacy concept with the mission of profit-with-purpose. Anyone who is involved with business sustainability and corporate governance, the financial reporting process, investment decisions, legal and financial advising, and audit functions will benefit from this book.

Keywords

business sustainability; financial economic sustainability performance; nonfinancial environmental, ethical, social, and governance sustainability performance; sustainability risk; sustainability disclosure; sustainability indexes; sustainability ratings; sustainability reporting; sustainability assurance; sustainability drivers; sustainability mandatory disclosures; sustainability voluntary disclosures; sustainability standard-setting organizations

Contents

Preface

Business sustainability has gained considerable attention of investors, regulators, standard-setters, business organization, academics, and the accounting profession in recent years. Business sustainability focuses on achieving financial economic sustainability performance to create shareholder value and desired financial returns for shareholders while securing social and environmental impacts. The primary purpose of business sustainability is to create shared value for all stakeholders from shareholders to employees, customers, suppliers, creditors, society, community, and the environment. This book examines three sustainability factors of performance, risk, and disclosure.

This book consists of four chapters covering all three sustainability factors with a keen focus on its implications for business organizations. Anyone who is involved with business sustainability and corporate governance, the financial reporting process, investment decisions, legal and financial advising, audit functions, and corporate governance education will be interested in this book. Specifically, corporations, their executives, the boards of directors, board committees, internal and external auditors, accountants, lawmakers, regulators, standard-setters, users of financial statements (investors, creditors, and pensioners), investor activists, business schools, and other professionals (attorneys, financial analysts, and bankers) will benefit from this book. This book offers guidance for proper measurement, recognition and reporting of all five economic, governance, social, ethical, and environmental (EGSEE) dimensions of sustainability performance. Sustainability performance and accountability reporting have gained a new interest in the aftermath of 2007–2009 Global Financial Crisis and the 2020 COVID-19 pandemic and resulted global economic meltdown, which has sparked widening concerns about whether big businesses are sustainable in the long term in contributing to the economic growth and prosperity of the nation. The ever-increasing erosion of public trust and investor confidence in the sustainability of large businesses, the widening concern about social responsibility and environmental matters, overconsumption of natural resources, the global government bailout of big businesses, and the perception that government cannot solve all problems of businesses underscore the importance of keen focus on sustainability performance, risk, and disclosure.

The primary theme of this book is on the examination of business sustainability performance, risk, disclosure reporting, and assurance and their integration into strategy, governance, risk assessment, cost management, performance management, and the reporting process of disclosing governance, ethical, social, environmental, and economic sustainable performance. This book also highlights how people, business, and resources collaborate in a business sustainability and accountability model. This book is intended to cover a variety of issues relevant to business sustainability and their implications for organizations of all types and sizes. I hope you find this book relevant and useful to gain and maintain your business and personal sustainability.

Zabihollah (Zabi) Rezaee
November 3, 2020

Acknowledgments

I acknowledge the Securities and Exchange Commission, the Public Company Accounting Oversight Board, the American Institute of Certified Public Accountants, the Big Four Accounting Firms and Corporate Governance Organizations, American Accounting Association, Global Reporting Initiative (GRI), International Integrated Reporting Council (IIRC), Sustainability Accounting Standards Board (SASB), United Nations, and other sustainability standards-setting organizations for permission to quote and reference their professional standards and other publications.

The encouragement and support of my colleagues at the University of Memphis are also acknowledged. Especially, my graduate assistant, Ms. Naomi Riley for providing invaluable assistance. I thank the members of the Business Expert Press team and Exeter Premedia for their hard work and dedication in editing the book, including, Scott Isenberg, John Wood, and Dhinesh Kumar.

My sincere thanks are due to my family, my wife Soheila, and my children Rose and Nick. Without their love, enthusiasm, and support, this book would not have come to fruition when it did. I am dedicating this book to the loving memory of my sister Monireh Rezaee and my younger brother Heshmat (John) Rezaee.

CHAPTER 1

An Introduction to Business Sustainability

Executive Summary

Business sustainability is rapidly and newly advancing from the greenwashing and branding to the business imperative as investors demand, regulators require, and companies present their sustainability factors of performance, disclosure, and risk. Investors are demanding public companies to disclose nonfinancial environmental, social, and governance (ESG) sustainability performance information in addition to financial economic sustainability performance (ESP) information to enable them to assess the risks associated with the companies' operations and performance. Regulators worldwide including the Securities and Exchange Commission (SEC) in the United States require public companies to disclose ESG information in their regulatory filings. Business sustainability has become an economic and strategic imperative with potential to create opportunities and risks for businesses in creating shared value for all stakeholders. This book examines sustainability factors of performance, risk, and disclosure. The five dimensions of business sustainability performance are economic, governance, social, ethical, and environmental (EGSEE) dimensions. Sustainability risks include reputational, strategic, operational, compliance, and financial (RSOCF) risks among others. Sustainability disclosures are relevant to all five EGSEE dimensions of sustainability performance.

This introductory chapter provides a synopsis of all three factors of business sustainability. Chapter 2 presents sustainability performance whereas Chapters 3 and 4 focus on sustainability risk and disclosure, respectively. These chapters address the increasing focus on business sustainability and its factors of performance, disclosure, and risk and their implications for policy consideration, business practice, education, and research.

Introduction

There have been considerable efforts to encourage business organizations to pursue profit-with-purpose goals and for investors to integrate financial economic sustainability performance (ESP) and nonfinancial environmental, ethical, social, and governance (EESG) sustainability performance into their strategic and investment decisions. The nonfinancial EESG sustainability performance is often summarized as environmental, social, and governance (ESG) sustainability performance with ethics integrated into other sustainability dimensions. This book presents five dimensions of business sustainability performance as economic, governance, social, ethical, and environmental (EGSEE) and further classifies the dimensions to financial ESP and nonfinancial EESG sustainability performance. This introductory chapter provides a synopsis of all three business sustainability factors of performance, risk, and disclosure whereas Chapters 2 through 4 describe these factors in more depth and scope.

This chapter presents guidelines for proper measurement, recognition, and reporting of all five EGSEE dimensions of sustainability performance. Sustainability performance and accountability reporting have gained a new interest in the aftermath of 2007–2009 Global Financial Crisis and the resulting global economic meltdown, which has sparked widening concerns about whether big businesses (banks and car makers) are sustainable in the long term in contributing to economic growth and prosperity of the nation. The challenges brought on by the 2020 COVID-19 pandemic has caused business organizations to pay more attention to their sustainability, survival, and continuity as well as to take care of their employees, suppliers, and customers while creating shared value for all stakeholders.

Business Sustainability: Definition and Relevance

Business sustainability has been defined in many ways. It has been defined from agency/shareholder theory as the process of creating and maximizing shareholder wealth by aligning management interests with those of shareholders. In this regard, the main purpose of business sustainability is to enable management to focus on short-, medium-, and long-term strategic decisions to achieve high performance in creating shareholder value.

Business sustainability can be defined from the legal and compliance view as the process of complying with all applicable laws, rules, regulations, and standards including those related to the environment and society in achieving all five EGSEE dimensions of sustainability performance. Until recently, the terms "business sustainability," "corporate social responsibility" (CSR), and "triple bottom line" (focusing on profit, people, and planet) have been used interchangeably in the literature and authoritative reports. However, the concept of business sustainability is broader than just CSR and thus a more comprehensive definition of sustainability has been developed.

Business sustainability, for the purpose of this book, is defined as a process (journey) of achieving financial economic sustainability performance (ESP) in generating value for shareholders (desired returns on investment) while achieving nonfinancial EESG sustainability performance in creating shared value for all stakeholders (having social and environmental impacts).[1] In this chapter, business sustainability focuses on generating financial ESP to create shareholder value while achieving nonfinancial EESG sustainability performance in protecting interests of other stakeholders including creditors, customers, employees, suppliers, government, society, and the environment.[2]

The term CSR has evolved over the years. Originally, CSR referred primarily to philanthropy, good community relations (in a general sense), and employee engagement activities. While many researchers and companies still use CSR in that sense, it has evolved to a more holistic meaning—one where stakeholders are emphasized over shareholders, and corporate performance is assessed against EESG factors of performance, risk, disclosure, and their related metrics. The challenge is that companies and academics use both definitions interchangeably today. Sustainability factors are more specific, though they are also subject to different

---

[1] This definition of business sustainability and factors of performance, risk and disclosure are adapted from Rezaee, Z., and T. Fogarty. 2019. *Business Sustainability, Corporate Governance, and Organizational Ethics*. Hoboken, NJ: Wiley.

[2] Much of discussion in this chapter and next three chapters comes from Rezaee, Z., and T. Fogarty. 2019. *Business Sustainability, Corporate Governance, and Organizational Ethics*. Hoboken, NJ: Wiley.

interpretations as sustainability includes financial economic sustainability and nonfinancial EESG factors. As sustainability truly becomes embedded into strategic plans and core business operations, a more standard and uniformly accepted definition and factors of sustainability will evolve.

Recently on August 19, 2019, the Business Roundtable (BRT) announced the adoption of a new Statement on the Purpose of a Corporation that promotes the move toward sustainability of creating shared value for all stakeholders.[3] The COVID-19 pandemic forces organizations to pay more attention to EESG sustainability by focusing on the safety, health, and well-being of their employees, suppliers, and customers.[4] Asset managers (e.g., Blackrock, State Street, and Vanguard) invest in sustainable companies with social responsibility focus and take EESG sustainability factors of performance, risk, and disclosure into consideration when making investment decisions.[5] Investors, in the aftermath of the COVID-19 pandemic, public health, economic situation, and social justice crises, are paying more attention to the EESG factors and have intensified their focus on sustainability and business continuity. The amount of ESG funds available to U.S. investors has increased substantially in 2019 to $20.6 billion, about four times more than the amount of funds invested in ESG in 2018.[6]

The World Economic Forum (WEF 2020), in defining the purpose of a business organization, states, "A company is more than an economic

---

[3] Business Roundtable (BRT). 2019. "Statement on the Purpose of a Corporation." August 19, 2019. Available at https://opportunity.businessroundtable.org/wp-content/uploads/2019/09/BRT-Statement-on-the-Purpose-of-a-Corporation-with-Signatures-1.pdf

[4] Rezaee, Z., and N. J. Rezaee. 2020. "Stakeholder Governance Paradigm in Response to the COVID-19 Pandemic19 Pandemic." *Journal of Corporate Governance Research* 4, no. 1.

[5] Investor Responsibility Research Center Institute (IRRCi). 2018. "Measuring Effectiveness: Roadmap to Assessing System-level and SDG Investing." https://irrcinstitute.org/wp-content/uploads/2018/03/FINAL-TIPP-Report-Measuring-Effectiveness-Report-2018.pdf (accessed on July 14, 2018).

[6] Lacurci, G. 2020. "Money Moving into Environmental Funds Shatters Previous Record." *CNBC*, January 14, 2020. Available at https://cnbc.com/2020/01/14/esg-funds-see-record-inflows-in-2019.html

unit generating wealth. It fulfills human and societal aspirations as part of the broader social system. Performance must be measured not only on the return to shareholders, but also on how it achieves its environmental, social, and governance objectives."[7] Thus, the purpose of business organizations has transformed from profit maximization and shareholder wealth creation to generation of shared value for all stakeholders.

The ever-increasing erosion of public trust, social trust, and investor confidence in the sustainability of large businesses, the widening concern about social responsibility and environmental matters, social unrest, overconsumption of natural resources, the global government bailout of big businesses, and the perception that government cannot solve all problems of businesses underscore the importance of keen focus on business sustainability and the improvement of ESGEE. Sustainability risks are reputational, strategic, operational, compliance, and financial (RSOCF). Sustainability disclosures are relevant to financial ESP and nonfinancial ESG sustainability performance with ethics integrated into all other components of sustainability performance. Throughout the book we use ESG and environmental, ethical, social, and governance (EESG) interchangeably. The next section presents business sustainability initiatives as a framework and guidelines for the discussion of sustainability factors of performance, risk, and disclosure.

The Government Accountability Office (GAO) analyzed EESG sustainability disclosures of 32 large and mid-sized public companies in 2020 to determine why investors obtain EESG disclosures, what EESG sustainability factors are, and what advantages and disadvantages of ESG policy options are.[8] The 2020 GAO report indicates that the majority of institutional investors obtain and use EESG information to better understand and assess risks that could affect companies' financial performance.[9]

---

[7] World Economic Forum. 2020. "Toward Common Metrics and Consistent Reporting of Sustainable Value Creation." January 2020. Available at https://weforum.org/agenda/2020/03/covid-19-personal-data-new-commodity-market/

[8] United States Government Accountability Office (GAO). 2020. "Report to the Honorable Mark Warner U.S. Senate. Public Companies Disclosure of Environmental, Social and Governance Factors and Options to Enhance Them." July 2020. Available at https://gao.gov/assets/710/707949.pdf

[9] Ibid.

Currently, a number of organizations are addressing these sustainability factors of performance, risk, and disclosure by establishing practices in terms of mandatory and voluntary initiatives. However, these initiatives are still constantly being evaluated, as their effectiveness are debatable. The next section provides a description of these initiatives and attempts to assess their relative success.

Business Sustainability Initiatives

In the aftermath of the 2020 global COVID-19 pandemic and the Global Financial Crisis of 2007–2009, business organizations are required to improve their performance in all five (EGSEE) dimensions of sustainability. At the same time, corporations are expected to effectively communicate their EGSEE sustainability performance to all their stakeholders through sustainability reporting. This section discusses drivers of recent moves toward business sustainability performance, integrated/sustainability, sustainability disclosure, risk assessment, reporting, and assurance. Responding to increasing interest in and demand for business sustainability factors of performance, disclosure, and risk as well as reporting by corporations, many public companies now voluntarily manage, measure, recognize, and disclose their commitments as well as events and transactions relevant to all five (EGSEE) dimensions of sustainability performance. The number of firms reporting sustainability has been increasing from 50 global companies two decades ago to more than 50,000 in recent years.

Sustainability initiatives are designed to maximize corporate social benefits and environmental impacts while minimizing the potential conflicts of interest among corporations, society, and the environment caused by the differences between private and social costs and benefits, and to align corporate goals with those of society. There are many examples of potential conflicts of interest between corporations and society, and some can be related to social injustice and unrest, environmental issues (pollution, acid rain, global warming), poor quality of education, child labor in developing countries, and wages paid by multinational corporations in poor countries. Business sustainability measures, which include rules, regulations, and best practices of CSR programs, can raise companies' awareness of the social costs and benefits of their business activities. The Organization for Economic Co-operation and Development (OECD) defines the purpose of a CSR program as, "To encourage the positive contributions that multinational enterprises can make to economics, environmental, and social progress and to minimize the difficulties to which their various operations may give rise."[10] This definition focuses on two important aspects of a CSR program, namely the creation of social value through corporate activities (social value-added activities) and the avoidance of conflicts between corporate goals and societal goals (societal consensus). These two aspects of CSR programs should be integrated into business sustainability strategies, decisions, performance, and reporting.

There are several mandatory and voluntary guidelines for sustainability factors of performance, risk, and disclosure including the reporting frameworks released by GRI, integrated reporting promoted by the International Integrated Reporting Council (IIRC), and the sustainability reporting guidelines of the Sustainability Accounting Standards Board (SASB). Research by the Callan Institute survey reported 43 percent of respondents have voluntarily incorporated ESG factors into the investment decision-making process and 8 percent of total respondents are considering incorporating ESG factors into future business decisions. Furthermore, these respondents that incorporated ESG into the investment decision-making process indicate that they will broaden their approach to ESG (39 percent) in the next one to three years, implying a continued progression of implementation.[11] An alternative to mandatory sustainability reports is to standardize the sustainability performance reporting and assurance by accomplishing the following:

(a) Provide an intellectual framework in core principles and objectives of sustainability that guide standard-setting efforts in modernizing and standardizing sustainability reporting and assurance.

---

[10] Organisation of Economic Co-operation and Development (OECD). 2003. "Guidelines for Multinational Enterprises." Available at www.oecd.org

[11] Callan Institute. "2013 Survey. ESG Hitting Its Stride in U.S." July 2018. Available at https://callan.com/esg-survey-2018/

(b) Offer a common language of the standardized sustainability reports that improve the ability of standard setters to communicate ideas and intentions with key stakeholders.

(c) Standardize sustainability performance reports, risk assessment, disclosures, and ratings.

(d) Establish globally accepted reporting framework and standards for sustainability disclosures.

(e) Create uniformity in objectively measuring all five dimensions of EGSEE performance.

(f) Establish globally accepted and widely used sustainability key performance indicators (SKPI) for all five dimensions of sustainability performance.

(g) Develop a framework for proper assessment and management of all aspects of sustainability risks.

(h) Create uniform sustainability disclosure guidelines.

(i) Ensure that a wide range of stakeholders, including investors, have access to uniform and comparable sustainability reports.

(j) Establish standardized sustainability assurance processes.

(k) Establish sustainability disclosure index and ratings.

Mandatory Business Sustainability Initiatives

Countries that have adopted mandatory sustainability initiatives are Australia, Austria, Canada, Denmark, France, Germany, Malaysia, Netherlands, Sweden, Hong Kong, and the United Kingdom. These countries have adopted mandatory reporting on financial ESP and nonfinancial ESEG sustainability performance.[12] Corporate mandatory disclosures are designed to provide investors with relevant, useful, and reliable information in making sound investment decisions and thus vital to the financial market. In the context of the agency theory, moral hazard occurs in the presence of information asymmetry where the agent (management) acting on behalf of the principal (shareholders) knows more about its actions and/or intentions than the principal does because of

---

[12] Rezaee, Z. 2015. *Business Sustainability: Performance, Compliance, Accountability and Integrated Reporting.* Sheffield, UK: Greenleaf Publishing.

the lack of proper monitoring of the agent. When the interests of the agent are not aligned with those of the principal, the agent has incentives and may not act in the best interest of and/or withhold important information from the principal. In the case of mandatory disclosures, there are fewer opportunities for the existence of information asymmetry. As of now, there is no mandatory disclosure of sustainability performance information. Corporate disclosure, mandatory or voluntary, is the backbone of financial markets worldwide. Public companies are required to disclose a set of financial information if their securities are held by the public. The primary purpose of corporate disclosure is to provide economic agents (e.g., shareholders, creditors) with adequate information to make appropriate decisions. This financial information to investors protects their interests and enhance their confidence in the financial reports and markets, mitigating the information asymmetry associated with the agency problems, and ensuring that stock prices fully reflect all value-relevant information in an efficient capital market.

Business sustainability encourages management to manage earnings in different ways to meet the needs of a variety of stakeholders. A shareholder, for example, may believe that the purpose of the company is to create value in order to generate a desired return on investment. Customers, on the other hand, may expect that the company provides not only the product or service advertised, but also gives back to society in a meaningful way. Customer satisfaction, business reputation, brand value, environmental initiatives, and social responsibility are often considered as intangible business assets that cannot be described adequately in purely economic terms. Likewise, these assets and their value should be linked to their related economic value over the long term. Shareholders are better off in the long term by recognizing the various financial benefits derived from the intangible business assets generated through sustainability efforts and development. Thus, management should be motivated to achieve sustainable economic performance for shareholders while protecting the interests of other stakeholders. Mandatory disclosures are disclosures of information required by law or regulation. This sustainability information can occur within financial filings such as 10-Qs, Annual Reports, and Management Disclosure & Analysis or nonfinancial reports such as Health and Safety reports or Pollutant Release/Emissions reports.

EU Directive

In 2017 it became mandatory for the European Union (EU) companies to disclose nonfinancial ESG sustainability information under the Directive 2014/95/EU (EU 2014).[13] According to the EU Directive, transparency can be achieved through better disclosure practices, which leads to more sustainable firm policies. Disclosure of nonfinancial and diversity information by certain large undertakings and groups in annual reports. It was initially proposed by the European Commission in April 2013 and voted in Parliament in favor (599 to 55) on April 15, 2014. European Commission has adopted a directive that require more than 6,000 companies to disclose their environmental, social, governance, and diversity sustainability performance for the 2017 reporting year and onward.

The EU Directive is intended to increase transparency, improve ESG performance on environmental and social matters, and contribute effectively to long-term economic growth and employment. All publicly traded companies with at least 500 employees, banks, insurance companies, public-interest entities designated by national governments. Scope includes approximately 6,000 large companies and groups across the EU. Many entities are exempt from mandatory ESG disclosure requirements including small-medium enterprises (SMEs) with less than 500 employees, companies with annual reports relying on frameworks (such as the UN Global Compact, ISO 26000, the German Sustainability Code, or GRI guidelines) covering the information required.

The European Commission directive (1) requires companies to disclose their environmental, social, governance, and diversity sustainability performance; (2) is effective for the 2017 reporting year and onwards; and (3) affects over 6,000 companies. Companies must report

- Environmental performance
- Social and employee-related matters

---

[13] European Union (EU) Directive 2014/95/EU. "Directive 2014/95/EU of the European Parliament and of the Council amending Directive 2013/34/EU as Regards Disclosure of Non-Financial and Diversity Information by Certain Large Undertakings and Groups." Available at https://eur-lex.europa.eu/legal-content/EN/TXT/PDF/?uri=CELEX:32014L0095&from=EN

- Human rights policies
- Anticorruption and bribery issues
- Diversity on the board of directors
- Covered organizations will need to include information about their suppliers

Asset managers and investment advisers will be required to take the following steps to comply with the Disclosure Regulation:

- *Policies and Procedures.* To produce the required disclosures, in-scope firms will need to consider and document the relevance of ESG to their investment policies. In addition, when preparing or updating their staff remuneration policies (including, where required, public or investor disclosures with regards to their remuneration practices), managers will be required to specify how these policies are consistent with the integration of sustainability risks. This will involve making a series of strategic business and investor relations decisions.
- *Website Disclosures.* All managers will be required to publish on their websites information about their policies on integration of sustainability risks in their investment decision-making processes. Additional public disclosure obligations will apply to larger firms (with 500 employees or more) and will include descriptions of investment due diligence processes for assessing adverse impacts of investment decisions on sustainability factors, a description of the principal adverse sustainability impacts, policies on their identification and prioritization, any action taken or planned with regards to such sustainability impacts, as well as information on the manager's shareholder engagement policies. Firms that choose not to take sustainability risks into account when making their investment decisions will be required to provide clear reasons for their decision.
- *Precontractual Disclosures.* Disclosures on the manner in which sustainability risks are integrated into investment decisions and advice and the results of the manager's assessment of the

likely impacts of sustainability risks on the returns must also be included in the "pre-contractual disclosures," such as the investment management agreement relating to a separately managed account, or the private placement memorandum or prospectus of a fund. If a manager does not consider sustainability risks to be relevant, the precontractual disclosures must include a clear explanation of the manager's rationale.

- *Sustainable Investments.* Additional detailed disclosure obligations will apply to investments that are marketed as sustainable investments (meeting the requirements of the Taxonomy Regulation) or other products that promote specific ESG characteristics.

Hong Kong Exchange

The listed companies in Hong Kong have played an important role in promoting and implementing business sustainability integrated reporting. The Hong Kong Stock Exchange (HKEX), in 2015 issued the Environmental, Social and Governance (ESG) Reporting Guide that requires listed companies to disclose ESG information on a comply-or-explain basis effective from financial years ending on or after December 31, 2015.[14] The Hong Kong Stock Exchange code provisions for sustainability reporting are detailed in Appendix 24: Environmental, Social and Governance (ESG) Reporting Guide of the Hong Kong Stock Exchange Listing Rules for the Main Board, listing companies HKLR Appendix 27 has come into effect since January 2016, and the HKEX issued "7 recommendations" in ESG disclosure in May 2018, followed by other updates in November 2018.

The "Environmental" subject area includes three aspects: emissions (A1), use of resources (A2), and the environment and natural resources (A3). The "Social" subject area includes eight aspects: employment (B1),

---

[14] Hong Kong Stock Exchange (HKEX). 2018. "Exchange Publishes Its Latest Review of Listed Issuers' Corporate Governance Practices and Updates Its Guidance Material On ESG Reporting." *HKEX*, www.hkex.com.hk/News/News-Release/2018/181116news?sc_lang=en

health and safety (B2), development and training (B3), labor standards (B4), supply chain management (B5), product responsibility (B6), anticorruption (B7) and community investment (B8). Each "aspect" contains both "comply or explain" items and "recommended disclosure" items. The growing popularity of ESG disclosures comes in part due to global market competition and mainly from the future sustainability benefits. China is the world's largest developing country and has been the leader in introducing many sustainability policies such as ESG guidelines. Research on the interactive effect between ESG and green innovation and its impact on firm value from the perspective of information disclosure focuses on the Hong Kong Stock Exchange ESG disclosures.[15] This research finds the following conclusions: (1) Green innovation plays a stronger role in promoting medium- and high-level firm value. (2) In terms of environment, information disclosure can only significantly promote low-level firm value.[16] The positive impact of social information disclosure on firm value is stronger with the increase of firm value level, and the negative impact of governance information disclosure on firm value is stronger with the increase of firm value level.

SEC and Sustainability Disclosures

SEC regulations on firm valuations and corporate ESG policies have drastically changed in the past 50 years due to globalization, technological advancements, and other industry-specific developments. A study on the SEC regulations and their relationship with firm value was done to identify the benefits and detriments to these increasingly

---

[15] February 24, 2020. "The Ubteraction Effect between ESG and Green Innovation and Its Impact on Firm Value from the Perspective of Information Disclosure." *Economic Business Aspects of Sustainability* 12, no. 5. Available at https:// mdpi.com/2071-1050/12/5/1866/htm

[16] Coluccia, D., M. Dabić, M. Del Giudice, S. Fontana, and S. Solimene. 2020. "R&D Innovation Indicator and Its Effects on the Market. An Empirical Assessment from a Financial Perspective." Available online https://sciencedirect.com/ science/article/pii/S0148296319302577

stringent rules on the marketplace.[17] The research finds that firms that increase their demand for SEC regulatory compliance have correlation to increased regulatory burdens. Regulations were thus found to have stronger impacts than deregulations, which is consistent with the theory that increased regulatory burdens push out weaker companies thus increase the power of other companies. Firms are in effect, more likely to leave the market or end in bankruptcy with increasing SEC restrictions. Overall, the effects of SEC regulations are crucial to shaping the corporate sector and determining the outcomes of firm existence.

The SEC concept on disclosure reform was released on April 22, 2016, which includes 11 pages of discussion of sustainability disclosure, and poses the following questions:[18]

1. How sustainability disclosure fits within the existing regulatory requirements (Regulation S-K)?
2. What is the current cost of sustainability disclosure?
3. What are the challenges with line-item requirements?
4. How can a market standard for sustainability disclosure benefit companies?
5. Should the focus be on ESG sustainability disclosures or just environmental and climate change matters?

The SEC Investor Advisory Committee has held multiple discussions on the topic of ESG Disclosures in regard to business sustainability. The use of ESG-related disclosures has gone from a simple concept to a mainstream global investment priority. This points toward a global convergence

---

[17] SEC Regulations and Firms. March 2020. "Stern School of Business." Available at https://poseidon01.ssrn.com/delivery.php?ID=22100000209312306912111 61011020640090260350410770880700770100910680930761210820 99113107032044122020126111018115115114087107113022032092 07903 61251000891171210750790790230080771181250650300670670260 89003 1141071240040841160971120150800871010050650680790 05&EXT=pdf
[18] Securities and Exchange Commission (SEC). 2016. "Business and Financial Disclosure Required by Regulation S-K." Release No. 33–10064; 34–77599; File No. S7-06-16, Available at https://sec.gov/rules/concept/2016/33-10064.pdf

of investor interest in these ESG disclosures. For these reasons and more, the Advisory Committee recommends the following:

1. Investors require reliable, material ESG information upon which to base investment and voting decisions.
2. Issuers should directly provide material information to the market relating to ESG issues used by investors to make investment and voting decisions.
3. Requiring material ESG disclosure will level the playing field between issuers.
4. The United States should take the lead on disclosure of material ESG disclosure. Issuers are taking a variety of approaches to provide this ESG related information to investors.

At the Meeting of the Asset Management Advisory Committee, Chairman Clayton stated:

I look forward to hearing from the Committee's recently-formed subcommittees focused on private investments and on environmental, social, and governance (or, "ESG") issues. I have spoken at length on issues in both areas. I believe I have made it clear that, while I believe that in many cases one or more "E" issues, "S" issues, or "G" issues are material to an investment decision, I have not seen circumstances where combining an analysis of E, S, and G together, across a broad range of companies, for example with a "rating" or "score," particularly a single rating or score, would facilitate meaningful investment analysis that was not significantly over-inclusive and imprecise. I have requested engagement on this topic, particularly from active portfolio managers with actual track records, and I greatly appreciate your efforts to inform the Commission in this area.

European ESG Initiatives

On November 27, 2019, the European Parliament and the Council of the European Union passed disclosure regulations relevant to ESG information for the financial sector.[19] The UN General Assembly adopted a new global sustainable development framework: the 2030 Agenda for Sustainable Development (the "2030 Agenda"), which includes the Sustainable Development Goals (SDGs) at its core. The recent European regulations on ESG disclosures will take effect on March 10, 2021, and will enhance the reliability and transparency of ESG disclosures and their valuable contribution to investment decisions and other proposals.[20] Research shows that these diverging measures will continue to be adopted at the national level and possibly in different approaches in various financial service sectors that might persist. The regulation aims to reduce information asymmetries in principal–agent relationships with regard to the integration of sustainability risks, the consideration of adverse sustainability impacts, the promotion of environmental or social characteristics, and sustainable investment, by requiring financial market participants and financial advisers to make precontractual and ongoing disclosures for investors when they act as agents of those end investors. Overall, the new requirements are comprehensive and are likely to encourage corporates to have the best practices that would ultimately incentivize adopting firms to increase their ESG sustainability disclosure.

Regulators in the UK and the EU have recently proposed additional ESG disclosures to promote sustainable economic activity. For example, the UK's Financial Conduct Authority (FCA) published a consultation paper, in March 2020, proposing that certain UK firms make climate change disclosures.[21] Disclosure policies of enterprises should include, but not be limited to, material information on: (a) the financial and operating results of the enterprise; (b) enterprise objectives; (c) major

---

[19] The European Parliament and the Council of the European Union (EDR). 2019. "Regulations on Sustainability-related Disclosures in the Financial Services Sector." *Official Journal of the European Union*, December 12, 2019. Available at https://eur-lex.europa.eu/eli/reg/2019/2088/oj

[20] Ibid.

[21] United Kingdom's Financial Conduct Authority (UK/FCA). 2020. "Proposals to Enhance Climate-Related Disclosures by Listed Issuers and Clarification of Existing Disclosure Obligations." *Consultation Paper*, March 2020, Available at https://wlrk.com/docs/FCA_-_Consultation_Paper.pdf

share ownership and voting rights, including the structure of a group of enterprises and intragroup relations, as well as control enhancing mechanisms; (c) remuneration policy for members of the board and key executives, and information about board members, including qualifications, the selection process, other enterprise directorships, and whether each board member is regarded as independent by the board; (e) related party transactions; (f) foreseeable risk factors; (g) issues regarding workers and other stakeholders; and (h) governance structures and policies, in particular, the content of any corporate governance code or policy and its implementation process. Enterprises should install high-quality standards for accounting and financial, as well as nonfinancial disclosure, including environmental and social reporting. In addition, the standards or policies under which information is compiled or published should be reported.

Many enterprises have taken a step further and adopted measures designed to help them comply with the law and standards of business conduct, and to enhance the overall transparency of their operations. An increasing number of firms have issued voluntary codes of corporate conduct, which are expressions of commitments to ethical values in such areas as environment, human rights, labor standards, consumer protection, or taxation. Specialized management systems have been, or are being developed, and continue to evolve with the aim of helping respect these commitments of information systems, operating procedures, and training requirements. Firms are encouraged to provide simple and economical access for all to published information and to consider making use of information technologies to meet this goal. Information that is made available to users in home markets should also be available to all interested users in other markets. Furthermore, firms may have to take special steps to make information available to communities that do not have access to printed media.

Organization for Economic Co-operation and Development (OECD) Guidelines

The OECD Guidelines are recommendations addressed by various governments, specifically toward multinational enterprises involving sustainability. The OECD Guidelines have a main objective to ensure that operations of each enterprise is in harmony with the related and current government policies with the purpose to strengthen the basis of mutual confidence between the enterprises and society, to improve the foreign investment environment, and to enhance the contribution to sustainable development by enterprises. In the modern world, service and knowledge-intensive industries are on the rise, quickly expanding with the aid of the Internet economy, service, and technology enterprises. The online economy is playing an increasingly crucial role in business sustainability and the OECD Guidelines have evolved to reflect these changes in the marketplace. The speed, nature, and scope of these economic changes have presented challenging strategies for enterprises and their stakeholders. Some firms have responded to public concerns by improving or creating internal programs for guidance and support for management systems to enhance their commitment to good corporate citizenship, business, practices, and internal conduct.

The OECD Guidelines have contributed to business sustainability in important ways, such as through the development of standards that cover sustainable areas involving the environment, carbon footprint, fraudulent reporting risks and corruption, consumer interests and desires, as well as corporate governance mechanisms and diversity. The common goal of businesses to adhere to the OECD Guidelines is to encourage positive contributions to business sustainability for the economy, environment, and social progress and to minimize sustainable difficulties. In reaching this goal, governments can help by providing effective domestic policy frameworks to included sustainability, stability in the long run, impartial system of courts and laws, appropriate regulation, and efficient and honest public administration. Governments can also aid by promoting the appropriate sustainability standards and policies to support the development while also engaging ongoing current reforms to ensure that the public sector is contributing actively, efficiently, and effectively. The businesses and governments adhering to the OECD Guidelines are more committed to the continuous improvement of sustainability policies with an aim and perspective to improve the welfare and living standards of all people and future peoples.

OECD General Policies

1. Contribute to economic, environmental, and social progress with a view to achieving sustainable development.
2. Respect the internationally recognized human rights of those affected by their activities.
3. Encourage local capacity building through close cooperation with the local community, including business interests, as well as developing the enterprise's activities in domestic and foreign markets, consistent with the need for sound commercial practice.
4. Encourage human capital formation, in particular by creating employment opportunities and facilitating training opportunities for employees.
5. Refrain from seeking or accepting exemptions not contemplated in the statutory or regulatory framework related to human rights, environmental, health, safety, labor, taxation, financial incentives, or other issues.
6. Support and uphold good corporate governance principles and develop and apply good corporate governance practices, including throughout the enterprise groups.
7. Develop and apply effective self-regulatory practices and management systems that foster a relationship of confidence and mutual trust between enterprises and the societies in which they operate.
8. Promote awareness of and compliance by workers employed by multinational enterprises with respect to company policies through appropriate dissemination of these policies, including through training programs
9. Refrain from discriminatory or disciplinary action against workers who make bona fide reports to management or, as appropriate, to the competent public authorities, on practices that contravene the law, the guidelines, or the enterprise's policies.
10. Carry out risk-based due diligence, by incorporating it into their enterprise risk management systems, to identify, prevent, and mitigate actual and potential adverse impacts and account for how these impacts are addressed. The nature and extent of due diligence depend on the circumstances of a situation.

11. Avoid causing or contributing to adverse impacts on matters covered by the Guidelines, through their own activities, and address such impacts when they occur.

12. Seek to prevent or mitigate an adverse impact where they have not contributed to that impact, when the impact is nevertheless directly linked to their operations, products, or services by a business relationship. This is not intended to shift responsibility from the entity causing an adverse impact to the enterprise with which it has a business relationship.

13. In addition to addressing adverse impacts in relation to matters covered by the guidelines, encourage, where practicable, business partners, including suppliers and subcontractors, to apply principles of responsible business conduct compatible with the guidelines.

14. Engage with relevant stakeholders in order to provide meaningful opportunities for their views to be taken into account in relation to planning and decision making for projects or other activities that may significantly impact local communities.

15. Abstain from any improper involvement in local political activities.

In addition to the OECD Guidelines, enterprises should take into account the already established accounting policies in the country that they operate as well as consider the views of other investors and creditors. The OECD Guidelines further encourage enterprises to: (1) support, as appropriate to their circumstances, cooperative efforts to promote Internet Freedom through respect of freedom of expression, assembly, and association online and (2) engage in or support, where appropriate, private or multistakeholder initiatives and social dialogue on responsible supply chain management while ensuring that these initiatives take due account of their social and economic effects on developing countries and of existing internationally recognized standards.[22]

---

[22] "OECD Guidelines for Multinational Enterprises." 2011 edition. OECD. Available at https://oecd.org/daf/inv/mne/oecdguidelinesformultinational enterprises.htm

In summary, mandatory sustainability initiatives require companies to report:

- Environmental performance
- Social and employee-related matters
- Human rights policies
- Anticorruption and bribery issues
- Diversity on the board of directors
- Covered organizations will need to include information about their suppliers.

Voluntary Initiatives

Several organizations worldwide including the Global Reporting Initiative (GRI), International Integrated Reporting Council (IIRC), Sustainability Accounting Standard Board (SASB), and the United Nations Global Compact have issued guidelines regarding voluntary disclosure of sustainability performance information. These guidelines have been used by over 15,000 public companies in producing stand-alone integrated sustainability reports. This subsection summarizes these sustainability-related guidelines and their issuing organizations.

Global Reporting Initiative

The Global Reporting Initiative (GRI) is an international independent standards organization and its sustainability reporting and disclosure standards are most widely used standards for reporting on nonfinancial ESG sustainability performance. GRI global sustainability reporting standards have been developed through multistakeholder participation and they address both comprehensive ESG reports and selected disclosures. GRI standards provide disclosure guidelines for companies to communicate their ESG sustainability performance including environmental issues of climate change, social issues of human rights, and governance issues of board diversity and independence. GRI establish globally accepted sustainability standards to promote sustainable development, advance sustainability initiatives, guide effective and efficient sustainability reporting, and enable appropriate use of sustainability information to improve ESG sustainability performance.

The GRI was launched in 1997 to bring consistency and global standardization to sustainability reporting. The evolution of GRI guidelines began with the initial focus on incorporating environmental performance into corporate reporting with its first publication, Sustainability Reporting Guidelines, in 2000.[23] The GRI was originally created in response to the demand for comparable sustainability reporting worldwide. These GRI Sustainability Reporting Guidelines are updated periodically to reflect new developments in sustainability reporting and guidance. Guideline G4, released in May 2013, is the fourth update so far. The G4 Guideline presents Reporting Principles, Standard Disclosures, and an Implementation Manual for sustainability reporting on economic, governance, social, and environmental sustainability performance metrics by all organizations regardless of their type, size, sector, or location.[24] It focuses more heavily on materiality considerations in the reporting process and final report. The intention is to make sustainability reports, "more relevant, more credible, and more user-friendly" by encouraging companies to center their reports on the organization's goals and the impacts it may have on society and other stakeholders. In this guideline, the GRI promotes sustainability reporting as a standard practice of disclosing sustainability-related issues that are relevant to companies' business and their stakeholders.

The G4 Guideline is broken into two parts: (1) "Reporting Principles and Standard Disclosures," which contains the criteria necessary for an organization to prepare its sustainability report "in accordance" with the Guideline, and (2) the "Implementation Manual," which instructs practitioners how to apply the Reporting Principles, how to prepare disclosure information, and how to interpret various concepts in the guideline.[25] There are also two components—Core and Comprehensive—for

---

[23] Global Reporting Initiative (GRI). 2013. "G4 Sustainability Reporting Guidelines." Available online at https://globalreporting.org/resourcelibrary/GRIG4-Part1-Reporting-Principles-and-Standard-Disclosures.pdf (accessed on March 29, 2016).

[24] Ibid.

[25] Ibid.

the "in accordance" process of identifying material to be disclosed under the concept "Aspects," under which refer to information with the most influential economic, environmental, and social impacts or have a marked effect on the decisions and perceptions of stakeholders. The "Core" information should be disclosed in all cases and is meant to serve as a background for disclosing the impacts of its performance in economics, governance, social, and environmental sustainability dimensions. The Comprehensive option requires additional Standard Disclosures on strategy and analysis, governance, and ethics and integrity, along with more extensive reporting on all "indicators" related to the material aspects identified earlier in the process, rather than the minimum of one required to be in accordance with the Core requirements.[26]

Global Sustainability Standards Board of the GRI

The Global Sustainability Standards Board (GSSB) has sole responsibility for setting the first globally accepted standards for sustainability reporting—the GRI Sustainability Reporting Standards. This was established as an independent operating entity under the auspices of GRI. The GSSB is formed by 15 members representing a range of expertise and multistakeholder perspectives on sustainability reporting. The GSSB operates under the GSSB Terms of Reference to oversee the development of the GRI Standards according to a formally defined due process.[27]

The GSSB works exclusively in the public interest and according to the vision and mission of GRI. With the exception of some administrative discussions, which can be held privately at the GSSB's discretion, all GSSB meetings are open to the public and available online. The GRI Sustainability Reporting Standards are the product of more than 15 years of robust, global, multistakeholder development. This development is governed by a formally defined Due Process Protocol, which is overseen by the Due Process Oversight Committee (DPOC). The Due Process Protocol is designed to ensure that the GRI Standards promote the public interest and are aligned with GRI's vision and mission. It also ensures that GRI Standards

---

[26] Ibid.

[27] Global Sustainability Standards Board. GRI 2020. Available at https://global-reporting.org/standards/gssb-and-standard-setting/

move through a clearly communicated development process. This starts with project identification, prioritization, and commencement; continues with content development, public exposure, and consideration of feedback; and concludes with the final release of Standards.[28]

International Integrated Reporting Council

The International Integrated Reporting Council (IIRC) is a global coalition of investors, public companies, regulators, standard setters, nongovernmental organizations (NGOs), the accounting profession, and academia. The coalition promotes communication about value creation as the next step in the evolution of corporate reporting. The IIRC's mission is to establish integrated reporting and thinking within mainstream business practice as the norm in the public and private sectors. The IIRC's vision is to align capital allocation and corporate behavior to wider goals of financial stability and sustainable development through the cycle of integrated reporting and thinking.[29] The IIRC has established the Integrated Reporting Framework that is intended to enable companies to produce a concise, standardized, and investor-focused sustainability reports. The integrated reporting framework enables companies to report their sustainability performance by focusing on six "capitals" (financial, manufactured, human, natural, intellectual, and social and relationship).

In April 2013, the IIRC released the draft of its framework consultation on integrated reporting intended to provide guidelines on communication with stakeholders.[30] The IIRC's proposed framework addresses fundamental concepts of integrated reporting and its guiding principles on an organization's strategy, governance, performance, and prospects.

---

[28] Global Sustainability Standards Board. Due process development. GRI 2020. Available at https://globalreporting.org/standards/gssb-and-standard-setting/due-process-development/

[29] Integrated Reporting IR. International Framework revision Consultation Draft and Companion Document. May 2020. Available at https://integrated reporting.org/resource-type/technical/

[30] International Integrated Reporting Committee (IIRC). 2013. "IIRC Consultative Draft.2013." *IIRC Consultative Draft Section* 3.12; p. 19. http://theiirc.org/consultationdraft2013/

The IIRC, in its December 2013 Integrated Reporting Framework, promotes a more integrated approach to corporate reporting by improving the quality and quantity of information disseminated to providers of financial capital including shareholders and other stakeholders.[31]

Sustainability Accounting Standards Board

The Sustainability Accounting Standards Board (SASB) issues sustainability accounting standards to enable public companies to disclose material, relevant, and decision useful ESG information to investors by integrating ESG information into their mandatory filings. SASB is currently offering 77 different industry-specific standards for public companies. In October 2013, the SASB released its Sustainability Conceptual Framework consisting of objectives, key definitions, and characteristics of sustainability accounting and disclosures, methodology for assessing the materiality of sustainability issues, and structure and harmonization of sustainability accounting standards.[32] The SASB has developed sustainability accounting standards relevant to disclosing material sustainability issues for 88 industries in 10 sectors, launching the process for mandatory filings to the Securities and Exchange Commission (SEC) that enable comparisons between companies, which can be useful for investment decisions and allocations of capital. Harmonizing SASB standards with existing disclosure standards avoids additional costs for companies and aligns SASB's work with global corporate transparency efforts.

In 2017, SASB established a standards-setting group consisting of nine individuals to revise its conceptual framework to ensure that its standards are relevant and enable disclosure of useful sustainability information to investors.[33] Consistent with the conceptual frameworks of the Financial Accounting Standards Board (FASB) and the International Accounting

---

[31] Ibid.

[32] Sustainability Accounting Standards Board (SASB). 2013. "Conceptual Framework of Sustainability Accounting Standard Board." October 2013. Available at http://sasb.org/wp-content/uploads/2013/10/SASB-Conceptual-Framework.pdf

[33] Sustainability Accounting Standards Board (FBASB). 2017. SASB Conceptual Framework, February 2017. Available at https://sasb.org/wp-content/uploads/2020/02/SASB_Conceptual-Framework_WATERMARK.pdf

Standards Board (IASB), the SASB's Conceptual Framework established the basic principles, objectives, and definitions that guide its technical staff in setting sustainability accounting standards. The proposed SASB's conceptual framework is still under revisions are intended to better articulate SASB's approach in setting sustainability accounting standards.

The proposed SASB's framework has substantially changed several aspects of the previous framework. First, the definition of the materiality is changed by specifying that SASB, "applies the definition of 'materiality' established under the U.S. securities law," suggesting that information is material if there is a "substantial likelihood that the disclosure of the omitted fact would have been viewed by the reasonable investor as having significantly altered the, 'total mix' of information made available." Thus, any sustainability disclosure is deemed material when it influences the decision of a reasonable investor in providing decision-useful and relevant information. Second, there are more clarity and guidelines on the characteristics of decision-useful information with the intent to provide more clarity in articulating principles that guide standards. Finally, the SASB's rules and procedures are revised, which affect the content of the future SASB's standards.

The SASB has recently launched a new certification for those who wish to obtain credentials in sustainability. The candidates can obtain Fundamentals of Sustainability Accounting (FSA) certification at two levels: Level I and Level II. The level I focuses on essential principles and emerging practices of sustainability, its learning objectives are to learn about the trends driving demand for sustainability performance, reporting, and assurance information, how to integrate sustainability information into managerial and investment decisions, SASB approaches to sustainability and how to integrate sustainability information to corporate reporting, the need for sustainability accounting, understanding SASB standards, and how to use SASB standards. The FSA Credential is designed for professionals who benefit from understanding the link between material sustainability information and a company's financial performance.

United Nations Global Compact

The 2013 Global Corporate (GC) Sustainability Report released by the United Nations Global Compact (UNGC) addresses the state of corporate sustainability today and presents the actions taken by companies worldwide in integrating sustainability to their strategies, operations, and culture. The report encourages companies to engage their suppliers in the establishment of more sustainable practices and integration of sustainability into their supply chain processes.[34] This establishment takes significantly more resources of various kinds to create efficient and effective sustainable practices in the supply chain process. Supply chains are a hurdle for sustainability reporting for large and growing companies. This is more likely due to the fact that many companies lack the implementing measures and reporting metrics to remediate their supply chain, rather than the actual supply chain itself.[35]

Global Compact participants rank supply chain practices as the largest challenge faced by firms in regard to improving their sustainability performance.[36] Many of the problems extend from the size of the supply chain, distance from suppliers, and operating with low standards. When organizations set a tone at the top to prioritize sustainability within the supply chain, progress can be made. The report finds that companies are increasingly focusing on business sustainability and making progress on setting expectations for their suppliers to integrate sustainability into their strategies and practices. Many large companies show significantly more effort in their commitment to action toward sustainability standards and therefore are also leading motivators. Some other benefits of sustainability reporting include improved reputation, increased employee loyalty, and higher customer satisfactions. However, there are several sustainability challenges that could be a threat to the business value if they

---

[34] United Nations Global Compact (UNGC). 2015. Guide to Corporate Sustainability. Available at https://unglobalcompact.org/docs/publications/UN_Global_Compact_Guide_to_Corporate_Sustainability.pdf(accessed on March 29, 2016).

[35] UN Global Compact Releases Sustainability Research Findings. TriplePundit. October 2013. Available at https://triplepundit.com/story/2013/un-global-compact-releases-sustainability-research-findings/48701

[36] Guide to Corporate Sustainability. Shaping a Sustainable Future. United Nations Global Compact 2020. Available at https://d306pr3pise04h.cloudfront.net/docs/publications%2FUN_Global_Compact_Guide_to_Corporate_Sustainability.pdf

are not addressed properly, but these challenges can also be turned into business opportunities.

According to the most recent update of Global Sustainability by the UNGC, over 12,000 organizations in over 160 countries are currently members of the global compact, with the majority coming from Europe and Latin America. The new guide presents performance of member organizations worldwide with respect to the 10 principles of the UNGC that are related to human rights, labor, environment, and anticorruption. The report indicates that investors continue to demand companies to act upon and report sustainability, while companies have found that it is beneficial to integrate corporate responsibility into their business operations. These new initiatives help to improve corporations' reputations and demonstrate that these corporations are active participants in the Global Compact, which in turn enhances stakeholder relations, improves commitment by the CEO, promotes internal information sharing, and provides information for investors.[37]

Principles of Responsible Investment

In 2005, the United Nations Secretary-General Kofi Annan invited a group of large institutional investors to join a process to develop the Principles of Responsible Investment (PRI), which was launched in April 2006, and the number of signatories has grown significantly from 100 to over 3,000.[38] The PRI addresses the long-term interests of its signatories and financial markets and economies as related to ESG sustainability factors of performance, risk, and disclosure and their integration into investment decisions. The PRI partners with the UN Environment Program Finance Initiative and the UN Global Compact to adopt and implement its six aspirational principles relevant to ESG such as the following:[39]

- Integrating ESG factors into investment analysis and decision-making processes

---

[37] Ibid.
[38] Principles for Responsible Investment (PRI). Available at https://unpri.org/pri/about-the-pri
[39] Ibid.

- Incorporating ESG factors into asset ownership policies and practices
- Obtaining disclosures on ESG issues by investee companies
- Advancing acceptance and implementation of the principles within the investment industry
- Promoting the effectiveness in implementing the principles
- Reporting on ESG activities and progress toward implementing the principles.

United Nations Sustainable Development Goals

In 2015, the UN General Assembly adopted 17 Sustainable Development Goals (SDGs) as part of its 2030 Agenda for Sustainable Development.[40] The 17 SDGs build on the United Nations Millennium Development Goals of 2000–2015 and involve new areas such as climate change, economic inequality, innovation, sustainable production and consumption, and peace and justice[41] (UNSDG 2015). These SDGs are relevant to the three dimensions of sustainability development, economic development, and social and environmental development and thus can be linked to ESP and ESG sustainability performance. The 17 SDGs address broad global goals such as no poverty (Goal 1), zero hunger (Goal 2), quality education (Goal 4), gender equity (Goal 5), responsible consumption and production (Goal 12), climate action (Goal 13), life on land (Goal 15), peace and justice (Goal 16), and partnerships for the goals (Goal 17). The SDGs are accompanied by a total of 169 associated targets and 232 approved indicators that are intended to be achieved by 2030. The SDGs are considered

---

[40] United Nations Development Program. 2020. "UNDP Launches Standards for Bond Issuers and Private Equity Funds Seeking SDG Impact." June 16, 2020, Available at https://undp.org/content/undp/en/home/news-centre/news/2020/UNDP_launches_standards_for_bond_issuers_and_private_equity_funds_seeking_SDG_impact.html

[41] UN Sustainable Development Goals report (UNSDGs). 2015. "Indicators and a Monitoring Framework for the Sustainable Development Goals Launching a data revolution for the SDGs." Available at http://unsdsn.org/wp-content/uploads/2015/03/150320-SDSN-Indicator-Report.pdf (accessed on 10 August 2017).

as a framework for prioritizing business sustainability strategies and related reporting and are being integrated into investment strategies.

Impact of COVID-19

The COVID-19 pandemic has caused an incredible impact on business environments and sustainability. Over the past decade, there has been an exponential growth in demand and supply for standard-compliant products therefore increasing the Voluntary Sustainability Standards (VSS) accordingly. Castka, Searcy, and Fischer study the initial responses to COVID-19 for these leading VSS group of 21 standards.[42] The intent of this research was to analyze data from various public sources to determine how each VSS has adjusted their certification services in response to COVID-19 pandemic travel bans and lockdowns, with a particular emphasis on the adoption of technologies. The findings show that remote working and information technology systems have a significant uptake and is not currently expected by VSS to extend beyond the pandemic crisis. The researchers go on to add that these changes may become adopted as the new normal and may even encourage businesses to utilize more advanced technology in certification services. Despite these overwhelming challenges that COVID-19 has created, businesses are demonstrating that they can take collective action to address these situations such as rapid implementation of remote working. Increased adoption of VSSs will ensure more efficient processes of certification services and ultimately increase the credibility and trustworthiness of businesses especially during the COVID-19 pandemic.

The manner in which companies are dealing with the regulations and other circumstances surrounding the pandemic reflects their true values and with the rise of social media influence. These actions will be publicly scrutinized, causing a more intense focus on sustainability and philanthropy. Another study by Main, Lindsay, and Hernandez[43]

---

[42] "Technology Enhances Auditing in Voluntary Sustainability Standards: The Impact of COVID-19." *MDPI Sustainability Journal*. June 2020. Available at https://mdpi.com/2071-1050/12/11/4740

[43] "Human Capital, Front and Center." *Harvard Law School Forum on Corporate Governance*. May 2020. Available at https://corpgov.law.harvard.edu/2020/05/14/human-capital-front-and-center/

probed the human capital relations and results from the COVID-19 pandemic. First, the research suggests that the social element, "S" in "ESG" (environmental, social, and governance) be moved to the forefront as social elements will become a top priority during COVID-19. The authors go on to say that business transparency will be key during and post-COVID-19 due to social norms and expectations. Social matters are mainly focused on employee layoffs and reductions, health and safety, employee engagement, and the role of executive leadership. While it is impossible to say exactly how COVID-19 will affect the future of business and social standards. it is reasonable to suggest that human capital issues will remain a focus of attention by the public.

Sustainability CFO and the Chief Sustainability Officer

The Institute of Management Accountants turns the attention to the role of corporate governance during and post-COVID-19. Gibassier, Arjalies, and Garnier[44] discuss how the role of the chief financial officer (CFO) will be adapted to reflect changes in the business environment due to the pandemic. The research suggests that a new job will appear in accounting practices labeled "Sustainability CFO." This new position will be a senior executive, reporting under the Chief Value Office or a related department, responsible for the sustainability performance, or the nonfinancial performance, of the company. Sustainability involves various departments and topics such as assessing social impacts and their effects on the firm's intangible assets, managing environmental carbon footprints, participating in corporate governance reporting standards, and more. For most firms, the true value of the organization significantly exceeds, what the financial statements report due to intangible assets. Those in the accounting field have struggled to accurately and consistently value this crucial nonfinancial information in reports. Research indicates that

---

[44] "Sustainability CFO: The CFO of the Future?" Institute of Management Accountants. The Association of Accountants and Financial Professionals in Business. 2020. Available at https://imanet.org/insights-and-trends/external-reporting-and-disclosure-management/sustainability-cfo-the-cfo-of-the-future?ssopc=1

80 percent of the valuation of a company actually depends on the worth of its intangible assets.[45]

Sustainability CFOs are accounting professionals that are usually CPA certified with extensive knowledge and experience who want to enhance the relationship between the firm's sustainability objectives and financial reporting. This goal will hopefully start the change into better inclusion of ESG disclosures while benefiting the day-to-day practices of the firm. The responsibilities and tasks of a Sustainability CFO are similar to those of the original CFO except with a focus on nonfinancial issues. The most important responsibility is reporting of nonfinancial information by using key performance indicators (KPI) as a performance measure and analyzing the results of ESG factors. In addition, Sustainability CFOs must conform to existing nonfinancial standards and regulations, become the link to "traditional" finance, and contribute in lobby and representation of accounting metrics for the future. Within these responsibilities, Sustainability CFOs will face challenges such as measuring sustainability and other intangible assets, choosing standards, and ultimately becoming a more competent sustainable accountant.

Chief sustainability officers (CSOs) are of critical importance to successful sustainability efforts and are often linked to environmental issues. Furthermore, the CSO contributes to the supply chain, improving working conditions, creating safety procedures, and more. The CSO can translate ESG business sustainability into corporate purpose, mission, and strategy that creates shared value for all stakeholders. The CSO should work with other executives and the board of directors in identifying and assessing sustainability factors of performance, risk, and disclosure.

The job brief of a CSO includes the following:

- Have profit-oriented mentality and practice. Seek profit from increasingly difficult avenues of growth.
- Be multidisciplinary in both their own knowledge and that of their staff.

---

[45] David Colgren, T. February 2017. "Expanding the Accounting Ecosystem." *Strategic Finance*, 62–63, http://sfmagazine.com/post-entry/february-2017-expanding-the-accounting-ecosystem/

- Find ways to reach out to new stakeholders or increase the participation of and communication with existing ones.
- Demonstrate flexibility in new endeavors that seek to increase the company's future growth aspects.
- Communicate effectively to other officers and employees about best practices in sustainability and enforce compliance with the same.
- Learn to leverage company strengths, such as technology, manpower, expertise, resources, and market positions.

Sustainability Performance

Business sustainability has gained significant attention from global investors, regulators, the business community, public companies, academics, and the accounting profession. More than 15,000 public companies worldwide are issuing sustainability reports on some or all five—economic, governance, social, ethical, and environmental (EGSEE)—dimensions of sustainability performance and this trend is expected to continue worldwide. Proper measurement of sustainability performance, as well as accurate and reliable disclosure of sustainability performance, and effective assessment of sustainability risks remain major challenges for organizations of different types and sizes. Different dimensions of business sustainability performance are considered in an isolated fashion, without effective integrations of both financial ESP and nonfinancial EESG sustainability performance and disclosures/reporting.

The process of disclosing economic, governance, social, ethical, and environmental (EGSEE) dimensions of sustainability performance separately and holistically is described in this section. The collaboration of people, business, and resources in business sustainability and accountability model along with best practices of business sustainability is explained. It also offers guidance to organizations to properly integrate all five EGSEE dimensions of sustainability into their business models, strategic plans, and practices. It also provides guidelines for complete and accurate measurement, recognition, and disclosure of all five EGSEE dimensions of sustainability performance in an integrated reporting model.

Business sustainability is a multidisciplinary and multidimensional concept with multiple users. This section considers different dimensions of business sustainability (economic, social, governance, ethics, and environmental sustainability) when analyzing their impacts on business practices and outcome holistically by considering the reciprocal relationship among all related parties. Business sustainability is often defined only in terms of one aspect of CSR and thus ignores regulations and practices related to other dimensions of sustainability. These incomplete definitions of business sustainability could not provide a complete picture of the underlying business practice and may provide incomplete yet biased conclusions. Attention is given to the interactions of all five EGSEE dimensions of sustainability performance and possible tensions among these dimensions. Economic sustainability performance is the primary dimension that practitioners should emphasize, while environment, social, and governance sustainability may interact with economic sustainability and produce important effects that should not be ignored. It provides descriptions of current practices of sustainability reporting and assurance and how these practices can enhance the overall concept of business sustainability practice and performance.

In this context, a model of business sustainability should incorporate activities that generate financial (long-term earnings, growth, and return on investment) and nonfinancial sustainability performance (governance, social, ethical, and environmental) that concern all stakeholders. In practice, business sustainability should be viewed as a collection of procedures that improve both financial ESP and nonfinancial EESG sustainability performance dimensions that create shared value for all stakeholders. Sustainability financial and nonfinancial performance is presented in detail in Chapter 2.

Sustainability Risk

The concept of business sustainability should be examined with respect to their practices, risk assessment reporting, and assurance concurrently. Due to the principal–agent relationships between managers and different stakeholders, the concept of business sustainability should be examined from the angles of these related parties simultaneously rather than in an isolated fashion. Thus, it is important to understand that certain practices are put into practice for the purpose of effective reporting as well as to facilitate assurance, although the associated cost with related practice could be slightly higher. The 2013 Global Corporate Sustainability Report released by the United Nations Global Compact addresses the state of business sustainability today and presents the actions taken by companies worldwide in integrating sustainability to their strategies, operations, management practices, and corporate culture.[46]

Sustainability risks present the likelihood that an organization is not meeting its financial ESP and nonfinancial EESG sustainability performance targets. Several important sustainability risks are strategic, operations, compliance, financial, and reputation. The most important risk relevant to business sustainability is strategic risk. Strategic risks reflect failure of strategic plans in achieving sustainability goals and these risks should be identified, assessed, and managed and minimized to achieve sustainability goals. Operations risks are also relevant financial ESP and nonfinancial EESG dimensions of sustainability performance, the integration of all sustainability performance dimensions into operating activities across operational units, operation technology, supply chain, information technology, and other functional areas. The financial risk of issuing materially misstated financial reports is detrimental to sustainability of corporations. The company's reputation and its related risk should be evaluated on an ongoing basis and any damages to the reputation be minimized. These and other sustainability risks are further described in detail in Chapter 3.

Sustainability Disclosure

Sustainability disclosures reflect sustainability reporting, ranking, rating, and indexing. The sustainability reporting refers to the ongoing process of promoting, measuring, recognizing, enforcing, reporting, and auditing sustainability performance in all five (EGSEE) dimensions of

---

[46] United Nations (UN). February, 2013. "How Investors are Addressing Environmental, Social and Governance Factors in Fundamental Equity Valuation." United Nations-supported Principles for Responsible Investment (PRI). Available at http://unpri.org/viewer/?file=wp-content/uploads/Integrated_Analysis_2013.pdf

sustainability.[47] Business organizations have traditionally reported their performance on economic affairs and their main focus on financial results have become irrelevant. In recent years, stakeholders, investors, regulators, global organizations, and the public at large have increasingly demanded information on both financial ESP and nonfinancial ESG key performance indicators (KPIs) in the platform of multiple bottom line (MBL) accountability and sustainability reporting. Sustainability performance and accountability reporting have gained a new interest during the recent Global Financial Crisis and resulting global economic meltdown, which has sparked widening concerns about whether or not big businesses (e.g., banks and carmakers) are sustainable in the long term in contributing to the economic growth and prosperity of the nation.

The ever-increasing erosion of public trust and investor confidence in the sustainability of large businesses, the widening concern about social responsibility and environmental matters, the overconsumption of natural resources, the global government bailout of big businesses, and the perception that the government cannot solve all problems in the businesses world underscore the importance of having a keen focus on sustainability performance and accountability reporting. The United Nations Global Compact in its 2013 Global Corporate Sustainability Report, while underscoring the importance of business sustainability, calls on corporations worldwide to integrate 10 principles of sustainability pertaining to environment, human rights, fair labor, and anticorruption into their strategies and operations.[48] Chapter 4 presents sustainability disclosures including reporting, assurance, ranking, indexing, and rating in detail.

Conclusion

The sustainability disclosure initiatives, whether mandatory or voluntary, are intended to reflect the financial, social, ethical, governance, and environmental impacts of a company's business operation and thus provide relevant

---

[47] Brockett, A., and Z. Rezaee. 2012. *Corporate Sustainability: Integrating Performance and Reporting.* New York, NY: Wiley.
[48] United Nations (UN). February, 2013. "How Investors are Addressing Environmental, Social and Governance Factors in Fundamental Equity Valuation." *United Nations-supported Principles for Responsible Investment (PRI).* Available at http://unpri.org/viewer/?file=wp-content/uploads/Integrated_Analysis_2013.pdf

and reliable financial and nonfinancial information for all stakeholders including investors. This chapter presents a synopsis of sustainability factors of performance, risk, and disclosure. There are debates among policymakers and scholars that international accounting standard-setters such as the Financial Accounting Standards Board (FASB) and International Accounting Standards Board (IASB) should issue accounting standards for proper disclosure of EESG sustainability information. Effective achievement of all five EGSEE dimensions of sustainability performance demands

- "tone at the top" commitments to business sustainability strategies and actions;
- commitment by the board of directors and top executives is essential in effectively coordinating all sustainability strategies and activities and successfully implementing sustainability strategies; and
- there is an urgent need for the establishment of the position of chief sustainability officer (CSO) in C-suite of business organizations.

Takeaways

- Define sustainability shared value creation in your organization.
- Identify and assess the positive and negative impact of trends shaping your organization's sustainability performance dimensions of EGSEE.
- Identify nonfinancial metrics on nonfinancial dimensions of sustainability performance (governance, social, ethical, and environmental).
- Link nonfinancial sustainability performance metrics to the sustainable financial success of the business.
- Integrate strategy, objectives, performance, risk, and incentives across financial and nonfinancial information dimensions of sustainability activities.
- Use holistic and integrated internal and external reports in effectively communicating your business sustainability strategic decisions, actions, and performance to both internal and external users of sustainability reports.

CHAPTER 2

Sustainability Performance Factor

Executive Summary

The three critical sustainability factors of performance, disclosure, and risk were introduced and synthesized in Chapter 1. This chapter addresses sustainability performance that can be classified into two broad categories of financial and nonfinancial dimensions. The financial sustainability performance is referred to as economic sustainability performance (ESP) and consists of long-term earnings and related cash flows and growth and innovation. The nonfinancial sustainability performance consists of environmental, ethical social, governance, and ethical (EESG) components in generating ethical, accountable, social, and environmental impacts. The achievements of both financial ESP and nonfinancial EESG sustainability performance has contributed to the creation of shared value for all stakeholders including shareholders, employees, creditors, suppliers, customers, society, government, and the environment.

Introduction

Business sustainability is a relatively broad concept that is related to the benefits of both internal and external stakeholders. These stakeholders are those who have vested interests in a firm through their investments in the form of financial capital (shareholders), human capital (employees), physical capital (customers and suppliers), social capital (the society), environmental capital (ecological), and regulatory capital (government). Stakeholders have a reciprocal relation and interaction with a firm in the sense that they contribute to the firm's value creation and in return their well-being is also affected by the firm. Three factors of business sustainability that can affect stakeholders' well-being are sustainability performance, sustainability disclosures/reporting, and sustainability risks all of which are important to stakeholder's knowledge. This chapter examines sustainability performance.

Sustainability Performance

The sustainability performance factor underscores that firms that focus on their nonfinancial performance including social and environmental performance, conduct their business ethically, and manage their activities more effectively with good corporate governance are more financially sustainable. The voluntary disclosure factor of sustainability performance posits that "sustainability-centric" firms that focus on achieving financial economic sustainability performance (ESP) and nonfinancial environmental, ethical, social, governance (EESG) sustainability performance have more incentives to disclose information that will differentiate themselves from "non-sustainability-centric" firms that often do not focus on financial ESP and nonfinancial EESG in order to avoid a bad reputation. Therefore, disclosure of voluntary nonfinancial EESG sustainability performance may signal management's commitment to transparency of both financial and nonfinancial performance and thus can affect information asymmetry and firm value. The sustainability risk factor determines stakeholder exposure to risks associated with failure to achieve sustainability performance.

Sustainability performance is typically classified into financial economic sustainability performance (ESP) and nonfinancial EESG sustainability performance with ethical performance often integrated into both financial and nonfinancial dimensions of sustainability performance.[1] Although business sustainability continues to evolve, several dimensions of sustainability performance pertaining to social and environmental initiatives have gained widespread global acceptance. These initiatives include important matters such as ethical workspace, customer satisfaction, just and safe working conditions, nondiscriminatory

---

[1] Much of discussions and materials for this section and the next two sections come from Rezaee, Z., and T. Fogarty. 2019. *Business Sustainability, Corporate Governance and Organizational Ethics*. Englewood Cliffs, NJ: Wiley.

fair wages, workplace diversity and inclusion, environmental preservation, clear air and water, minimum age for child labor, safe and quality products, concern for the environment, and fair and transparent business practices. It is, however, important to realize that each industry has its own applicable set of sustainability financial and nonfinancial key performance indicators (KPIs) relevant to both financial ESP and nonfinancial EESG sustainability performance. Each business organization must carefully identify its own social and environmental responsibilities and impacts given the context of the business culture in which it operates. The proper and relevant list of financial and nonfinancial sustainability KPIs depends on a variety of factors including those as industry, legal regimes, cultural diversity, corporate mission and strategy, corporate culture, political infrastructure, and managerial philosophy. The following sections describe each of the ESP and EESG sustainability performance dimensions in depth.

Financial Economic Sustainability Performance (ESP)

The most important and commonly accepted dimension of sustainability is "economic performance," which consists of various factors. The primary goal of any business organization is to create shareholder value through generating sustainable economic performance throughout the firm life. Business organizations should focus on activities that generate long-term corporate performance rather than short-term profit to enhance the overall firm value. The economic dimension of sustainability performance can be achieved when business organizations focus on long-term sustainability performance and continuous improvement in areas of effectiveness, efficiency, and productivity. In addition, long-term economic sustainability performance should also be communicated to shareholders through the preparation of high-quality financial reports that are readily accessible.

In a broader term and in compliance with G4 of the Global Reporting Initiative (GRI) Guidelines, the economic dimension of sustainability should reflect the financial strengths and concerns and an organization's economic impacts on its stakeholders, the environment, and society by showing how the economic status of stakeholders changes in response to the organization's activities.[2] Economic sustainability performance can be measured directly through financial activities between an organization and its stakeholders or indirectly through nonfinancial costs and benefits of economic relations and their effects on stakeholders in terms of generating desired rate of returns for shareholders while achieving social and environmental impacts.

Although the conventional measures of cash flows, earnings, and return on investment are essential in evaluating financial performance, they don't necessarily reflect sustainable performance and future growth. The key metrics and measures of economic sustainable performance as operational efficiency, customer satisfaction, talent management, growth, and innovation that should be derived from internal factors of strategy, risk profile, strengths and weaknesses, and corporate culture as well as external factors of reputation, technology, completion, globalization, and utilization of natural resources.[3] In the aftermath of the COVID-19 pandemic, business survival and continuity as well as safety, health, and well-being of all stakeholders, particularly investors, employees, suppliers, and customers are becoming more relevant and important. Business sustainability demands an integrated effort by management and a change in managerial focus on the short-termism of the tangible quick wins to the achievement of long-term, sustainable nonfinancial performance. Withstanding sustainability requires an innate understanding of both performance and risks and their integration into the corporate culture as well as management strategies, decisions, and actions. This integrated approach to sustaining business sustainability enables top management to compete in the global marketplace strategically and effectively.

---

[2] Global Reporting Initiative (GRI). (2013). G4 Exposure Draft. 2013. Frequently asked questions about the G4 Exposure Draft and the second G4 Public Comment Period. March 9, 2014. Available at: https://globalreporting.org/resourcelibrary/G4-ED-PCP2-FAQs.pdf

[3] KPMG. 2013. Beyond Quarterly Earnings: Is the Company on Track for Long-term Success? Spring 2013 Audit Committee Roundtable Report. Available at auditcommittee@kpmg.com

The KPMG 2013 Audit Committee Roundtable Report highlights the importance of long-term sustainable performance by suggesting that focusing on quarterly earnings can undermine a firm's long-term sustainable performance.[4] The KPMG report suggests the use of financial and nonfinancial key performance indicators (KPIs) and drivers of sustainable performance of operational efficiency, customer satisfaction, talent management, and innovation.[5] The regulatory process and compliance requires that each company create and enforce company-level disclosures of economic activities the company is involved with in promoting its ESP.[6] Turnover ratios are effective in creating a clear picture of where a company stands currently in relation to the taxonomy. This also allows investors to report their investments activities as a percentage that can be compared to similar industries. In contrast, capital expenditure gives the investor insight as to the direction and credibility of the strategies for the company. With this information, investors can analyze environmental and sustainability performance and strategies of the company. Many companies have mandated to disclosure against the regulations are also required to comply with the nonfinancial directive, which only requires disclosure to the extent of the firm's development, performance, and position in relation to industry environmental matters.[7] The achievement of financial economic sustainability performance is the main objective function for any business organization. The primary purpose of any business organization is to create shareholder value measured in terms of generating desired returns on investment in maximizing firm value.

---

[4] KPMG. 2013. Beyond Quarterly Earnings: Is the Company on Track for Long-term Success? Spring 2013 Audit Committee Roundtable Report. Available at auditcommittee@kpmg.com

[5] Ibid.

[6] TEG Final Report on Financing a Sustainable European Economy. EU Technical Expert Group on Sustainable Finance. Taxonomy. March 2020.

[7] EUR-Lex European Law. Directive 2014/95/EU of the European Parliament. October 2014. Available at https://eur-lex.europa.eu/legal-content/EN/ALL/?uri=CELEX:32014L0095

Nonfinancial Environmental, Ethical, Social, and Governance (EESG) Dimensions of Sustainability Performance

Nonfinancial dimensions of sustainability performance are divided into environmental, ethical, social, and governance (EESG) dimensions. In the 2020 KPMG audit committee agenda, the board brings attention to the newfound challenges of EESG for the audit committees of business organizations.[8] KPMG flags seven issues that the audit committees should address in the 2020 audit committee agenda, which include matters such as reassess the scope and quality of EESG/sustainability reports and disclosures, refocus standards on ethical compliance and whistleblower programs, and help ensure that internal auditors stay focused on critical risks specific for nonfinancial disclosures. Environmental, ethical, social, and governance (EESG) issues and reporting standards have been growing in importance for a range of stakeholders, from customers to regulators to employees and activists. In the age of technology and immediate information, investors are demanding more transparent and higher quality reports to aid their decision making, especially on topics such as environmental and social issues that seem particularly important to the rising generation of millennials.

The audit committee should serve as a starter to encourage boards of directors to focus on EESG data in this new light. KMPG survey research suggests that management should be a part of the discussion to support EESG reporting and disclosures to ensure the company has the necessary infrastructure to support EESG issues. In addition, companies should redirect their sustainability focus on ethics, compliance, and whistleblower programs to reduce global regulatory challenges and increase data privacy, financial services, and consumer protection regulations and more. "Tone at the top" and the "top-down approach" are growing increasingly imperative for companies to develop high ethical standards and expectations for their investors. In the age of social media, it is of vital importance that

---

[8] KPMG. Summer 2020. "On the 2020 Audit Committee Agenda. Board Leadership Center." Audit Committee Roundtable Report. Available at https://boardleadership.kpmg.us/content/dam/boardleadership/en/pdf/2019/on-the-2020-audit-committee-agenda.pdf

companies create a culture of integrity, legal compliance, and high ethical values for investors of all kinds. Furthermore, firms must take leadership and initiative to help ensure that the internal audit is focused on key risks for sustainability nonfinancial reporting. The audit committee should continue to work hand in hand with the chief risk officer and chief audit executive to identify the confinancial risks posing a threat to the company such as brand reputation, operations, as well as environmental and social strategies. The following section provides in-depth descriptions of these dimensions individually.

Environmental Dimension of Sustainability Performance

Sustainability performance with respect to the environmental dimension has been gaining an increasing amount of attention from investors, regulators, and the business community. This is in part due to stakeholders demanding reliable and more transparent information about the impacts of an organization's activities and operations on the environment beyond what is legislated by law. Corporations can no longer solely focus on corporate profitability while also ignoring their impacts on society and the environment. The environmental dimension of sustainability performance includes creating a better work environment, reducing the carbon footprint, improving air and water quality, and maximizing the positive effects of an organization on natural resources and the environment. Currently, there is a large number of global organizations trying to encourage corporations to consider their impacts on society and the environment when making business decisions. For example, the Coalition for Environmentally Responsible Economies (CERES) and the UN Environment Program, in collaboration with the UN Global Compact, promote environmental initiatives.[9]

These initiatives include those such as environmental disclosures related to climate risks and opportunities, law and regulatory enforcement, and climate science policy actions. In short, the current disclosure requirements for environmental risks and threats are inconsistently applied and often inadequate information is provided. Governments

---

[9] CERES and Environmental Defense Fund.

throughout the world are also instituting measures to ensure that the environment is better protected by the behest of society at large. For example, the Chilean government recently canceled a $10 billion dam project in Patagonia due in part to inadequate environmental impact assessments, and in part pressure from citizens who did not want the natural beauty and usability of their land to be devastated.[10] In this case, the government decided to forego the economic benefits of the project in consideration not only of the current impact it would have on the environment but also in light of future known and unknown ramifications.

Academic research shows that environmental sustainability through EESG disclosure can strengthen corporate sustainability performance.[11] The results show that environmental performance is significantly and positively associated with economic sustainability performance, specifically economic value and shared value. This falls in line with the fact that stakeholder theory and shared value theory are similar to EESG information disclosure, which is an important factor in enabling a competitive advantage and enhancing corporate sustainability performance. Finally, the environmental dimension consists of various topics such as energy use, treatment of animals, natural resource conservation, waste, and pollution. Those that are specific to the business organization industry or have the potential to interact with the business environment should be properly disclosed in the financial statements. Insufficient environmental information may cause investors to become misled about the true nature of the firm's environmental sustainability performance and thus their future bottom line earnings.

The International Organization for Standardization (ISO) released ISO 14000 providing a set of environmental standards, which requires management to conduct regular evaluations of the Environmental

[10] Ng, A., and Z. Rezaee. 2018. "The Emergence of Business Sustainability: Educational, Practical and Research Implications." In *Research Handbook of Finance and Sustainability*. Cheltenham, UK: Edward Elgar Publishing, https://doi.org/10.4337/9781786432636.00034

[11] Corporate Economic, Environmental, and Social Sustainability Performance Transformation through ESG Disclosure. 2020. Available at. https://mdpi.com/2071-1050/12/9/3910

Management System (EMS) to ensure that the system is realizing the set goals and missions of the environmental policies.[12] The ISO standards present guidelines for environmental management, accounting, reporting, and auditing. The main goal for management's review of the EMS is to identify deficiencies and take proper actions to improve environmental practices in the future. A company will benefit economically and socially through the implementation and continuous improvement of an EMS that is relevant, accurate, and sustainable in monitoring and developing environmental best practices, missions, and goals. Environmental key performance indicators (KPIs), global environmental initiatives, environmental management systems, environmental reporting, environmental assurance and auditing, and environmental best practices should be developed to ensure the achievement of environmental sustainability performance. The ISO Environmental Sustainability Standards are listed in Table 2.1.

Climate-related sustainability performance and risks can affect financial performance and risks. In October 2018, members of the Network for Greening the Financial System (NGFS) acknowledged that "climate-related risks are a source of financial risk. It is therefore within the mandates of central banks and supervisors to ensure the financial system is resilient to these risks."[13] Climate change is one of the many sources of structural change affecting the financial system; however, it has specific risks and must be treated differently than other financial risks. The NSFG goes on to describe these characteristics such as far-reaching impact in breadth and magnitude affecting economies worldwide, the uncertainty of the foreseeable nature, irreversibility of the effects of greenhouse gases combined with lack of matured technology, and dependency on short-term actions without considering the future impacts determined by actions taken today. While we are unable to predict the economic future and the financial impacts of climate change, NGSF recognizes that there

---

[12] International Organization for Standardization (ISO). ISO 14000 Family: Environmental Management. https://iso.org/iso-14001-environmental-management.html
[13] A Call for Action Climate Change as a Source of Financial Risk. Network for Greening the Financial System Executive Summary First Comprehensive Report. April 2019.

Table 2.1 *The International Organization for Standardization (ISO)*
Standards

ISO 14000	Environmental Sustainability Standards
ISO 14001	Environmental Management Systems—Specification with Guidance for Use
ISO 14004	Environmental Management Systems—General Guidelines on Principles Systems, and Supporting Techniques
ISO 14010	Guidelines for Environmental Auditing—General Principles
ISO 14011	Guidelines for Environmental Auditing—Audit Procedures—Auditing of Environmental Management Systems
ISO 14012	Guidelines for Environmental Auditing— Qualification Criteria for Environmental Auditors
ISO 14020	Environmental Labeling—General Principles
ISO 14021	Environmental Labels and Declarations—Self-declaration Environmental Claims—Guidelines and Definition and Usage of Terms
ISO 14022	Environmental Labels and Declarations—Self-declaration Environmental Claims—Symbols
ISO 14024	Environmental Labels and Declarations—Environmental Labeling Type 1—Guiding Principles and Procedures
ISO 14031	Environmental Management—Environmental Performance Evaluation—Guidelines
ISO 14040	Environmental Management—Life Cycle Assessment—Principles and Framework
ISO 14041	Environmental Management—Life Cycle Assessment—Goal and Scope Definition and Inventory Analysis.
ISO 14050	Environmental Management—Vocabulary

Environmental Key Performance Indicators (KPIs)

- Production and delivery of environmentally safer products by using biodegradable, nontoxic, and naturally derived materials in the production.

- Efficient and effective utilization of scarce natural resources like power, energy, and scarce natural materials.

- Efficient and efficient use of recycled materials.

- Leveraging technology to maximize utilization of scarce resources and replacement of non-renewable resources.

- Effective and efficient utilization of non-waste technologies.

- Minimization of the use of harmful and unsafe materials and products.

- Assessment of environmental risks and management of environmental risks including providing for appropriate insurance of risks and environmental remediation and disposal efforts.

• Environmental reporting that discloses environmental risk assessment and management, compliance with environmental requirements, and measurement of environmental liabilities.
• Environmental external auditing and assurance on environmental reports.
Environmental Management Systems (EMS)
• Appropriate tone at the top set by the board of directors and senior executives.
• The compliance board committee and/or compliance officers assigned the primary responsibility for the environmental performance of the operations within their control.
• Proper education of all employees regarding environmental laws regulations and best practices,
• Development of environmental policies and procedures in compliance with environmental rules and regulations.
• Assessment and management of environmental risks and evaluation of environmental performance on ongoing monitoring process.
• Certification of compliance with established operating environmental procedures.
• Establishment of an environmental audit program to ensure periodic review of environmental KPIs each operation.
• Proper disclosure of environmental policies, procedures, reporting, and auditing to all stakeholders.

is a strong risk that climate-related financial risks are not fully reflected in the financial statements. Therefore, there is a crucial need for global coordination to action and firm willingness to collectively lead the business world into a more sustainable economy.

The NGSF provides six recommendations for professionals to enhance their role in climate change and these are as follows: (1) integrating climate-related risks into financial stability monitoring and microsupervision, (2) integrating sustainability factors into own portfolio management, (3) bridging the data gaps between private and public information, (4) building awareness and intellectual capacity and encouraging technical assistance and knowledge sharing, (5) achieving robust and internationally consistent climate and environmental related disclosure, and (6) supporting the development of a taxonomy of economic activities.[14] There is still a significant amount of work to be done within

---

[14] Ibid.

financial systems and further technical work is being done by the NGFS to help correlate financial risks with climate change.

The Task Force on Climate Related Financial Disclosures issued a recommendations report in June 2017 to address the growing concern of potentially misleading financial disclosures. One of the most essential functions of financial markets is to set a price for risk using the relevant information to make decisions. However, there has been more focus on risks directly related to finances instead of environmental, social, and governance risks. The Task Force on Climate-related Financial Disclosures recommend four key features as follows: adoptable by all organizations, included in financial filings, designed to solicit decision useful, forward-looking information on financial impact, and a strong focus on risks and opportunities related to transition to lower-carbon economy.[15]

The SEC in the past several decades has considered whether ESG disclosure are material and relevant to be integrated into the SEC filings by public registered companies.[16] The emerging ongoing growth in the use of ESG information by investors has encouraged the SEC to address the mandatory ESG disclosures by (1) providing investors with the material, comparable, consistent ESG information to make investment and voting decisions; (2) offering public companies with a framework to disclose useful and material ESG information; (3) creating more comparability and consistency regarding the disclosure of ESG information; and (4) making the U.S. ESG disclosure requirement align with the rest of the world in creating a level playing field among public companies worldwide. The SEC Investor Advisory Committee has held several sessions on ESG disclosures by U.S. issuers.[17]

---

[15] Financial Stability Board (FSB). 2017. Final Report: Recommendations of the Task Force on Climate—Related Financial Disclosures, June 2017. Available at https://fsb-tcfd.org/wp-content/uploads/2017/06/FINAL-2017-TCFD-Report-11052018.pdf

[16] Securities and Exchange Commission, Modernization of Regulation S-K Items 101, 103, and 105, Release No. 33-10668 (August 8, 2019).

[17] SEC Investor Advisory Committee. Discussion Regarding Whether Investors Use Environmental, Social, and Governance (ESG) Data in Investment/Capital Allocation Decisions https://sec.gov/spotlight/investor-advisory-committee-2012/iac110719-agenda.htm

Ethical Dimension of Sustainability Performance

Ethics is defined as "a process by which individuals, social groups, and societies evaluate their actions from a perspective of moral principles and value."[18] The corporate culture of integrity, competency, fainnes, mutual respect, diversity, and inclusion create an ethical environment that provide incentives and opportunities for individuals to conduct their activities ethically while punishing and correcting them if they engage in unethical conduct. Corporate culture should create an ethical business environment in which all employees are encouraged and empowered to do the right thing and discouraged to engage in unethical activities. There is an emerging trend toward increased corporate accountability and ethical behavior, which is reflected in the role and relevance of business ethics and codes of organization conduct. However, diversity, cultural differences, the existence of various value systems, and the sensitivity of moral issues make it difficult to achieve a consensus on and central theme for ethics, ethical behavior, and ethical performance. Business organizations often have their codes of ethics that guide ethical behavior throughout the organization and create culture of responsibility, compliance, and accountability. Proper and effective ethical performance is important to any entity regardless of size and type and professional organizations have their own codes of ethics. The next paragraph presents one example of such codes of ethics.

On October 5, the International Ethics Standards Board for Accountants (IESBA) issued its revisions to the International Code of Ethics for Professional Accountants.[19] The revision recognizes that public trust and confidence in the accounting profession plays an important role in wide-ranging professional activities performing by accountants and that such confidence is based on the skills and values accountants bring to their professional activities.

---

[18] Cordiero, W.P. 2003. The Only Solution to the Decline in Business Ethics: Ethical Managers. *Teaching Business Ethics* 7, no. 3, pp. 265–77.

[19] The International Ethics Standards Board for Accountants (IESBA). 2020. Final Pronouncement: Revisions to the Code to Promote the Role and Mindset Expected of for Professional Accountants. October 5, 2020. Available at https://ethicsboard.org/publications/final-pronouncement-revisions-code-promote-role-and-mindset-expected-professional-accountants

Important items that the revisions address are:[20]

- Reinforcement aspects of the principles of integrity, objectivity, and professional behavior.
- Focusing on behavioral expectations of all professional accountants and public trust by requiring them to have an inquiring mind in undertaking their professional activities.
- Recognizing the importance of accountants being aware of the potential influence of bias in their judgments and decisions.
- Emphasizing the supportive role, the right organizational culture can play in promoting ethical conduct and business.

The Institute of Internal Auditors present the Code of Ethics to govern the behaviors and expectations of individuals and organizations in the conduct of internal auditing.[21] The ethical dimension of ESG Sustainability Performance relies heavily on the profession of internal auditing and the rules of conduct applies to these professionals. Internal auditors are expected to apply and uphold the principles of integrity to establish trust and reliance in judgments, objectivity to exhibit the highest level of professional evaluation, confidentially of value and ownership of client information, and competency used to apply knowledge, skills, and expertise in decision making. The Institute's Code of Ethics extends beyond the original definition of internal auditing to include two essential components: (1) principles that are relevant to the profession and practice of internal auditing and (2) rules of conduct that describe behavior norms expected of internal auditors, which aid in interpreting the principles. This Code of Ethics provides a guideline for senior management and internal auditors to follow to enhance the transparency of the ethical dimension of ESG Sustainability Performance.

---

[20] Ibid.

[21] Institute of Internal Auditors (IIA). 2019. "Implementation Guides: International Professional Practices Framework (IPPF) for The IIA's Code of Ethics and the International Standards for the Professional Practice of Internal Auditing." Available at https://na.theiia.org/standards-guidance/Pages/Standards-and-Guidance-IPPF.aspx

Social Dimension of Sustainability Performance

The social dimension of sustainability performance reflects the transformation of social goals into business practices that benefit an organization's stakeholders. Social performance measures an organization's social mission and its alignment with the interests and values that of the society in which they operate. The social dimension of sustainability performance ranges from ensuring the high quality of products and services, enhanced customer satisfaction, and improved employee health and well-being to adding a positive contribution to the sustainability of the planet and the quality of life for future generations.

Socially responsible investment (SRI) is becoming an increasingly important part of business these days. Though the mantra of business has been long to increase shareholders' profits, the advent of benefit corporations (or B-corporations) has brought with it a chance for shareholders to affect businesses' methods of doing business to increase their own desire for social change, not personal enrichment. The United Nations Principles of Responsible Investing (PRI) were initiated in 2005 to promote global investors to integrate ESG into their investment decisions.[22] Recently, under sustainable and socially responsible investing (SRI) principles, investors consider various sustainability issues in their investment analysis, since SRI increased by more than 22 percent to $3.74 trillion in managed assets during the 2010–2012 period.[23]

The United Nations Guiding Principles of Human Rights apply to all business organizations worldwide to enhance standards and practices relevant to business and human rights and thus contributing to a socially sustainable globalization.[24] These guiding principles address

---

[22] United Nations Principles of Responsible Investing (UN PRI). 2005. The Fresh Fields Report. Available at www.unepfi.org/fileadmin/documents/freshfields_legal_resp_20051123.pdf

[23] Social Investment Forum (SIF). 2012. 2012 Report on sustainable and responsible investing trends in the United States, US SIF foundation: The forum for sustainable and responsible investment (November 2012).

[24] United Nations Human Rights. 2011. "UN Guiding Principles on Business and Human Rights." Available at https://ohchr.org/documents/publications/guidingprinciplesbusinesshr_en.pdf

1. responsibilities of states to protect and fulfill human rights and fundamental freedoms;
2. the role of business organizations in fulfilling their social responsibilities by complying with all applicable laws, rules, and regulations relevant to human rights; and
3. the need for human rights and obligations to be implemented and enforced.

The European Union Taxonomy is arguably one of the most significant contributions to the fight for sustainability reporting.[25] This performance threshold tool enables companies, investors, and issuers to meet safeguards for sustainability reporting. The EU Taxonomy has three thresholds referred to as "technical screening criteria," which are as follows: (1) substantially contribute to one of the six environmental objectives, which include climate change mitigation, climate change adaption, sustainable and protection of water and marine resources, transition to a circular economy, pollution prevention and control, and protection and restoration of biodiversity and ecosystems; (2) do no significant harm to the other five environmental objectives and; (3) meet the minimum safeguards for the OECD Guidelines on Multinational Enterprises and the UN Guiding Principles on Business and Human Rights. The report demonstrates how social standards should be integrated into OECD Guidelines and in practice. Specifically, the OECD guidance for due diligence and responsible business conduct involves identifying and assessing adverse impacts, mitigating those adverse impacts, tracking the implementation and results, and finally communicating how the impacts were addressed. This cycle should be used to address the social risks of the business on a continuous basis. Investors and other stakeholders consider the social safeguards and risks a company faces including the amount and

---

[25] Financing Sustainable European Economy. 2020. "Technical Report. Taxonomy: Final Report of the Technical Expert Group on Sustainable Finance." March 2020. Available at https://ec.europa.eu/info/sites/info/files/business_economy_euro/banking_and_finance/documents/200309-sustainable-finance-teg-final-report-taxonomy_en.pdf

credibility of available information, the nature of the financial product, and the size of the company.

Governance Dimension of Sustainability Performance

Corporate governance performance reflects how business organizations are managed and operated to generate shared value for all stakeholders. The corporate governance structure consists of principles that guide corporate officers and executives in fulfilling their responsibilities, corporate governance functions, and mechanisms.[26] Corporate governance functions are oversight function delegated to the board of directors in protecting shareholder interests, managerial function given to executives in managing the organization for benefit of shareholders, and other functions such as internal and external auditing and compliance. Corporate governance mechanisms are internal and external multidimensional measures and it is important to take into consideration all measures when examining governance sustainability performance. The corporate governance landscape has also changed significantly in the aftermath of the global 2007–2009 financial crisis. The lack of effective corporate governance has been identified frequently as an overriding contributing factor in the Global Financial Crisis. For example, a rising trend in corporate governance is the matter of "Say on Pay." As businesses become more transparent in regard to their inner workings, not to mention the stark realization of the income gap brought to light throughout the Great Recession, shareholders are asking for more say in how companies reward their executives.

Over time, different internal and external corporate governance measures have been established by policymakers and regulators to improve the quality of corporate governance and as a result, these establishments enhance stakeholders' trust and investors' confidence in corporate sustainable performance and reporting. It is important to note that the governance dimension of sustainability performance is affected by legal, regulatory, internal and external mechanisms, and best practices to create shareholder value while protecting the interests of other stakeholders. For example, regulatory reforms are designed to

---

[26] Rezaee and Fogarty (2019).

improve the quality and effectiveness of corporate governance, which are demanded by the business community. In summary, effective corporate governance sustainability performance promotes accountability for the board of directors and executives, enhances sustainable operational and financial performance, improves the reliability and quality of financial information, and strengthens the integrity and efficiency of the capital market, which results in economic growth and prosperity for the nation.

Corporate governance measures are established and implemented to provide guidelines for corporate gatekeepers from the board of directors to management, accountants, auditors, regulators, policymakers, financial advisors, and legal counsel to fulfill their responsibility of working together in improving corporate governance performance. The effectiveness of corporate governance performance determines an organization success in achieving shared value for all stakeholders. The EU Taxonomy addresses governance metrics by recommending that companies apply corporate governance practices drawn from the OECD Principles of Corporate Governance.[27] This endorsement includes focusing the companies attention toward compliance with emerging topics such as human and labor rights as well as combating bribery and extortion and social injustice encountered in recent years.

Importance and Relevance of ESP and EESG Dimensions of Sustainability Performance

The integration of sustainability performance dimensions into corporate culture, business environment, and managerial strategic decisions can create sustainable performance and thus shared value for all stakeholders. The integration of the financial ESP and nonfinancial EESG dimensions of sustainability performance into managerial strategies and practices enables companies to conserve scarce resources, optimize production processes, identify product innovations, achieve cost efficiency and effectiveness, increase productivity, and promote corporate reputation. The report also encourages companies to engage their suppliers in the establishment of more sustainable practices and integration of sustainability

---

[27] Ibid.

into their supply chain processes. However, these sustainability activities may require considerable resource allocation that could conflict with shareholder wealth maximization objectives and forces management to solely invest in sustainability initiatives that would result in long-term financial sustainability.

Theoretically, managements' engagement in nonfinancial EESG sustainability activities, performance, and disclosure can be viewed as value-increasing or value-decreasing for investors. On one hand, companies that effectively manage their business sustainability improve EESG performance, enhance their reputation, fulfill their social responsibility, and promote a corporate culture of integrity and competency. On the other hand, companies can only survive and generate sustainable performance when they continue to generate profits and create shareholder value. Nonetheless, financial and nonfinancial EESG sustainability performance and disclosures supplement each other and are not mutually exclusive. Companies with effective governance, social and environmental responsibility, and high standards of ethics are expected to produce sustainable performance, create shareholder value, and gain investor confidence and public trust. Sustainability has gained the attention of global financial institutions and investors as they began to consider how EESG risks affect their investment portfolio value. A proper understanding of sustainability theories, standards, risk assessment, and performance has been a major challenge for companies in measuring, recognizing, and disclosing both financial ESP and nonfinancial EESG dimensions of their sustainability performance and for corporate stakeholders (including shareholders) in effectively using sustainability performance information in their investment valuations and portfolio analysis.

The proper establishment and implementation of business sustainability requires identification of all stakeholders and integration of all dimensions of sustainability performance to managerial processes. Companies should use a principles-based approach in integrating both financial ESP and nonfinancial EESG sustainability information into their managerial processes from purchasing and inbound logistics, production design, and manufacturing process to distribution, outbound logistics, customer services, and social and environmental initiatives. However, these sustainability activities may require considerable resource allocation that could conflict with shareholder wealth maximization objectives and forces management to solely invest in sustainability initiatives that would result in long-term financial sustainability.

Business sustainability enables management to focus on long-term and enduring financial and nonfinancial performance and disclose high-value and forward-looking information to all stakeholders. Under business sustainability management, managers can gather and use relevant financial ESP and nonfinancial EESG information for planning and forecasting purposes. At the same time, they can focus on and improve the related metrics that drive the business. Through business sustainability, management can better focus on sustainable value-deriving activities and use sustainability information to effectively communicate the company's sustainability performance that creates value for stakeholders. Business sustainability promotes business strategy, planning and decision making, supply chain, and financial and nonfinancial management. It is important to communicate sustainability performance information regarding business profit, processes, people, and planet (the environment) to all stakeholders in an integrated sustainability report. The next section presents how all five EGSEE dimensions of sustainability performance can be disclosed in an integrated sustainability report that benefits all stakeholders.

The concept of sustainability performance suggests that management must extend its focus beyond maximizing short-term shareholder profit by considering the impact of its operation and entire value chains on all stakeholders including the community, society, and the environment. Disclosure of financial ESP and nonfinancial EESG dimensions of sustainability performance while signaling management commitments to sustainability and establishing legitimacy with all constituencies poses a cost–benefit trade-off that has implications for investors and business organizations. In creating stakeholder value, management should identify potential social, environmental, governance, and ethical issues of concern and integrate them into their strategic planning and managerial processes. There are many reasons and justifications of why management should integrate sustainability performance to its processes and practices including the pressure of the labor movement, development of moral values and social standards, and the change in public opinion about the role of business, environmental matters, governance, and ethical scandals.

Companies that are, or aspire to be, leaders in sustainability are challenged by raising public expectations, increasing innovation, continuous quality improvement, effective governance measures, high standards of ethics and integrity, and heightened social and environmental problems. Thus, management should develop and maintain proper sustainability programs that provide a common framework for the integration of financial ESP and nonfinancial EESG dimensions of sustainability to their management processes that consist of:

- Integration of financial and nonfinancial sustainability KPIs into the business and investment analysis, supply chain management, and decision-making process.
- Communication of the company's management sustainability strategies, practices, and expectations to major stakeholders including suppliers and customers to mitigate risks and foster corporate values and culture.
- Continuous assessment of the company's sustainability initiatives and related managerial processes to monitor and improve sustainability performance and identify challenging areas and risks that need further improvements.
- Promotion of product innovation and quality, customer retention and attraction, employee satisfaction and talent attraction, and productivity through management sustainability processes.
- Development of the environmental, social, ethical, and governance initiatives that will impact the company's ability to generate sustainable financial performance for shareholders and create value for all stakeholders.
- Establishment of financial and nonfinancial KPIs relevant to ESP and EESG dimensions of sustainability performance that support management strategic decisions and actions.
- Develop integrated sustainability reports to ensure that relevant financial and nonfinancial sustainability performance information is disclosed to all stakeholders.
- Prepare periodic certifications of both financial and nonfinancial sustainability KPIs, issuance of integrated sustainability

reports, and securing external assurance reports on financial ESP and nonfinancial EESG dimensions of sustainability performance.

The true measure of success for corporations should be determined not only by their reported earnings, but also by their governance, social responsibility, ethical behavior, and environmental performance. Business sustainability has received considerable attention from policymakers, regulators, and the business and investment community over the past decade and it is expected to remain the main theme for decades to come. Sustainability theories, standards, policies, programs, activities, risk management, and best practices presented in this book should assist business organizations worldwide to integrate five EGSEE dimensions of sustainability performance to their management processes to improve their KPIs as well as the quality of financial and nonfinancial sustainability information disseminated to their stakeholders.

Business sustainability requires business organizations to refocus their business purpose to create shared value for all stakeholders. Business organizations should expand their mission to not only generate profit and create shareholder value but also ensure shared value for all stakeholders. The concept of shared value challenges the way we think about profits, philanthropy, sustainability, and development. Sustainable shared value creation enables business organizations to integrate financial ESP with nonfinancial EESG into business culture and corporate environment. Shared value initiatives can be created in three ways: (1) producing products and services that increase shareholder wealth and meet societal needs including improved nutrition, education, health, and general well-being; (2) redefining productivity in the supply chain by investing in training and resources to create high-quality suppliers and improve ESP and ESG sustainability performance ; and (3) developing material indicator taxonomies to effectively measure revenue, costs, and value of the organizations.

The emerging business sustainability requires management to simultaneously consider divergent economic, governance, social, ethical, and environmental issues. Stewardship theory enables management to effectively exercise stewardship over a broader range of financial and nonfinancial assets and capital including financial, physical, human, social, and environmental capital. Stewardship among other theories enable firms and their management to translate ESG sustainability performance to financial performance and thus firm value creation. The relationships between business, society, and the environment are complex and often tense, and management must find ways to address the potential tension and maximize both financial and ESG sustainability performance. However, a single, cohesive, and integrated theory of business sustainability is lacking in explaining the multidimensional and apparently conflicting aspects of sustainability performance. Management is generally responsible for stewarding corporate resources including assets and capitals with an ethical vision toward how to benefit the broader range of stakeholders including society and the environment. Thus, management should not impose its vision of "good" on society but instead seek compliance with regulatory measures and the best practices of sustainability in creating shared value for all stakeholders. Regardless of which theory is more relevant to a particular firm or perhaps integrated theories can be more effective, management should effectively address climate change and other environmental challenges.

As stewards of business resources, management's primary role is to design and implement strategies that create shared value for all stakeholders by improving sustainability performance. Sustainability enables management to continuously improve performance by addressing business challenges in managing both opportunities and risks. Stewardship theory can provide a means by which management can engage with all stakeholders and focusing on the achievement of long-term improvements for financial ESP and nonfinancial EESG sustainability performance.

Management should not impose its vision of "good" on society, but instead seek compliance with regulatory measures and the best practices of sustainability. However, a stewardship mindset requires that management strategies and actions be focused on the continuous improvement of both financial ESP and nonfinancial ESG components of sustainability performance. Specifically, the rationales for promotion of management stewardship in business sustainability are:

1. Focus on business sustainability tends to align with the goal of long-term shared value creation for all stakeholders.

2. Sustainability can be achieved through effective practices of corporate operations, risk management, governance, and compliance.
3. Ineffective stewardship and unsustainable performance can contribute to loss of value for all stakeholders including shareholders.

Conclusion

Sustainability is taking center stage in business worldwide, particularly in the aftermath of 2020 global COVID-19 pandemic as businesses in response to and attempt to survive and take care of the safety, health, and well-being of their employees, customers, suppliers, and other stakeholders. Global investors demand financial economic sustainability performance (ESP) and nonfinancial environmental, ethical, social, and governance (EESG) sustainability performance information and regulators require the disclosure of such information. Sustainability is a process of achieving both financial ESP and nonfinancial EESG dimensions of sustainability performance to create shared value for all stakeholders. Business sustainability has advanced from a focus on CSR to integration into organizations' environment, strategic plan, business culture, and practices for achieving long-term and multidimensional EGSEE sustainability performance. This chapter addresses business sustainability performance as generating financial economic sustainability performance (ESP) to create value for shareholders, while achieving nonfinancial environmental, ethical, social, and governance (EESG) sustainability performance in protecting the interests of other stakeholders.

Takeaways

- Business sustainability is advancing from greenwashing and branding to, very recently, business imperative with integration into the business model, corporate culture, and strategic plan.
- There is a growing demand by investors for relevant and reliable nonfinancial EESG information for making investment decisions in the aftermath of 2020 global COVID-19 pandemic.

- Build awareness of growing sustainability opportunities and challenges.
- Integrate financial ESP and nonfinancial EESG dimensions of sustainability performance into your strategic plans, business processes, and supply chain.
- Incorporate the sustainability performance strategy into the overall corporate strategy including operational processes.
- Tell your success sustainability performance stories and best practices of sustainability performance.

CHAPTER 3

Sustainability Risk Factor

Executive Summary

The previous chapter describes the sustainability performance factor and this chapter focuses on the business sustainability risk factor. The second factor of business sustainability is sustainability risk of failure to achieve financial economic sustainability performance and non-financial environmental, ethical, social, and governance sustainability performance, which is important to all stakeholders, particularly investors in the assessment of their investments. Several risks are associated with business sustainability including strategic, operations, compliance, financial, and reputation. Four more emerging risks that currently is threatening sustainability of all types and sizes of organization are risk of potential cyberattacks and security breaches and the 2020 COVID-19 pandemic, climate change, and litigation risks. Consideration of and proper assessment and management of those nine risks are becoming increasingly important and play an effective role in achieving financial and nonfinancial sustainability performance. This chapter presents these nine sustainability risks in detail.

Introduction

Sustainability risks reflect the likelihood that an organization is not meeting its sustainability performance targets of achieving financial economic sustainability performance (ESP) and nonfinancial environmental, ethical, social, and governance (EESG) sustainability performance. Several risks are relevant to business sustainability including strategic, operations, compliance, financial, and reputation.[1] The 2020 Government Accountability Office (GAO) report indicates that many of the surveyed institutional investors integrate environmental, social, and governance (ESG) factors of performance and risk into their portfolio decisions to better understand risks associated with financial performance and information.[2] Investors, in general, use EESG disclosures provided by public companies to monitor management and assessment of EESG risks and to make investment and voting decisions. The most important risk relevant to business sustainability is strategic risk. Strategic risks should be identified, assessed, and managed with a keen focus on minimizing their negative effects and building up on the opportunities provided by addressing these risks.

Operations risks are also relevant financial ESP and nonfinancial EESG dimensions of sustainability performance, the integration of all sustainability performance dimensions into operating activities across operational units, operation technology, supply chain, information technology, and other functional areas. Many companies are facing the challenges of complying with these regulatory measures and noncompliance may cause significant risks of interruption and/or discontinuation of their business. Compliance risks need to be assessed, managed, and their negative impacts be minimized to attain sustainability performance. To achieve this objective, many companies have created either the board compliance committee or an executive position as compliance and risk officer. All financial ESP and nonfinancial EESG dimensions of sustainability performance are associated with business reputation, customer satisfaction, and the ethical workplace. The company's reputation and its related risk should be evaluated on an ongoing basis and any damages

---

[1] Brockett, A., and Z. Rezaee. 2012. "Sustainability Reporting's Role in Managing Climate Change Risks and Opportunities." In *Managing Climate Change Business Risks and Consequences: Leadership for Global Sustainability*, 143–58. Palgrave Macmillan.

[2] United States Government Accountability Office (GAO). 2020. Report to the Honorable Mark Warner U.S. Senate. Public Companies Disclosure of Environmental, Social and Governance Factors and Options to Enhance Them., July 2020. Available at https://gao.gov/assets/710/707949.pdf

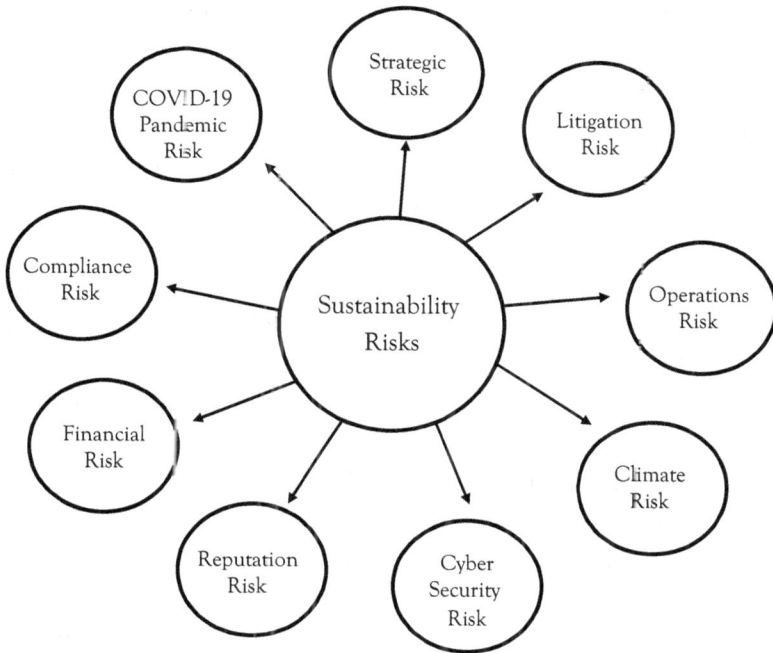

Figure 3.1 Sustainability risks

to reputation be minimized. The financial risk of issuing materially mis-stated financial reports is detrimental to sustainability of corporations. Sustainability reports are expected to be value-relevant to both external and internal users of such reports. Cyber hacking and security breaches of information systems are becoming a reality for many business (e.g., Sony, Target, Morgan Chase) and their risk assessment and controls demand significant IT investment and commitment by directors and offices to prevent their occurrences. This chapter present sustainability risk factors as depicted in Figure 3.1.

Sustainability Risks

Businesses are constantly changing and becoming more volatile, unpredictable, and complex, particularly during and in the aftermath of COVID-19 pandemic. In this challenging business environment, identification and assessment of risks are crucial to business survival, continuity, and sustainability. Investors typically consider sustainability risks when integrating financial ESP and nonfinancial EESG sustainability performance into their investment decisions. The majority of responding investors to a survey reported that consideration of nonfinancial EESG sustainability issues reduce investment risk and other drivers are enhancing performance and avoiding firms with unsustainable performance and unethical conduct.[3] Among several sustainability risks considered by investors are regulator noncompliance, cyberbanking, social unrest, the 2020 COVID-19 pandemic, reputational, changes in consumer preferences, and operational risks. These and other sustainability risks are presented in this section.

The International Organization for Standardization (ISO) published its new standard: ISO 31000: Risk Management—Principles and Guidelines in 2009, which provides principles and guidelines on risk management.[4] These ISO 31000 risk guidelines assist business organizations in developing, implementing, maintaining, and assessment, monitoring, and continuously improving their risk management system in minimizing the negative effects of strategic, operations, financial, compliance, and reputation risks.[5] These risks are interrelated and thus should be properly assessed and managed. For example, an excessive strategic risk can also cause operations, financial, compliance, and reputational risks. The compliance risk directly or indirectly associated with business sustainability, including noncompliance with regulatory reforms, health and safety, human rights and labor laws, corporate governance measures, anti-bribery, and environmental risks can vary among organizations and across countries. For example, environmental risks can include direct effects (e.g., emissions trading cost exposures) and indirect consequences

---

[3] PricewaterhouseCoopers (PwC). May 2014. "Sustainability goes Mainstream: Insights into Investor Views." http://pwc.com/us/en/pwc-investor-resource-institute/index.jhtml

[4] International Organization for Standardization (ISO). 2009. *ISO 31000: Risk Management–Principles and Guidelines, 2009. ISO.* www.iso.org (accessed July 31, 2011).

[5] Ibid.

(e.g., energy price increases and accompanying reporting and compliance costs) of noncompliance with environmental laws, rules, and regulations. Business organizations are also assessed and manage their financial risk of producing and disclosing materially misstated financial reports. Minimization of the reputational risk is vital to the success of sustainability programs and related performance, as stakeholder satisfaction is essential to sustainable business. The following subsection examines seven sustainability risks in detail as depicted in Figure 3.1.

Strategic Risk

The achievement of both financial ESP and nonfinancial EESG sustainability performance requires business organizations to strategically consider many sustainability factors that have strategic impacts and risks. There are several strategic risks triggered by business sustainability performance, reporting, and assurance, including threats to survival and achievement of long-term performance, uncertainty with marketing position and volatility in security prices, abnormal changes in consumer demand, risks associated with strategic investments, stakeholder communications, and investor relations. Of course, these strategic risks also create opportunities for possible improvements in operating, investing, financing activities, and proper communication with all stakeholders. Strategic risks should be identified, assessed, and managed with a keen focus on minimizing their negative effects and building up on the opportunities provided by addressing these risks. A recent research highlights the importance of enterprise risk management (ERM) in assessing and managing the strategic risk associated with sustainability performance implementation and sustainability reporting as the moderator between that and the business performance relationship and the moderating effect of sustainability reporting practices on the risk assessment.[6]

---

[6] Shad, M.K., F.W. Lai, C.L. Fatt, J.J. Klemeš, and A. Bokhari. 2019. "Integrating Sustainability Reporting into Enterprise Risk Management and Its Relationship with Business Performance: A Conceptual Framework." *Journal of Cleaner Production* 208, pp. 415-425. Available at https://sciencedirect.com/science/article/abs/pii/S0959652618331366

Operations Risk

Operations risks are associated with both financial ESP and nonfinancial EESG dimensions of sustainability performance, the integration of all sustainability performance dimensions into operating activities across operational units, operation technology, supply chain, information technology, and other functional areas. One of the greatest challenges for companies in implementing their sustainability strategy revolves around collaboration and integration across operational business units and key functional areas. Operational risks associated with both conventional financial key performance indicators (KPIs), such as earnings and return on investment, and nonfinancial KPIs, such as social and natural performance, need to be assessed, managed, and their negative impacts be minimized. These risks are related to the business operation impact on sustainability performance including those risks associated with IT, supply chain, and production facilities. Sustainability reporting can be used as a tool for more effective risk management and in identifying opportunities and risks associated with operations. The more transparent sustainability reporting is within operations risk the lower the risk of regulatory actions, higher customer confidence, and more effective management practices within the organization. As business sustainability and its reporting evolves, senior management and board directors will have to give considerable attention to the operations risk management and its overall effectiveness and efficiency.

Compliance Risk

Business organizations are required to comply with a set of local, national and international laws, rules, regulations, standards, and best practices. Compliance risks are those pertaining to failures to comply with local, national, and international laws, rules, regulations, and standards, dealing with issues ranging from the climate change to social responsibility and financial activities.[7] Many companies are facing the challenges

---

[7] Corporate Sustainability: Integrating Performance and Reporting. Brockett and Rezaee. Available at: https://books.google.com/books?hl=en&lr=&id=E K1NFc8kWZIC&oi=fnd&pg=PP13&dq=Operations+Risk+egsee+sustainab ility+performance&ots=8wiMqc3Hig&sig=OtcLSX8reP_VQNrju9zJnT-X_ q0#v=snippet&q=Operations%20Risk%20&f=false

of complying with these regulatory measures, and noncompliance may cause significant risks of interruption and/or discontinuation of their business. Compliance risks need to be assessed, managed, and their negative impacts be minimized. To achieve this objective, many companies have created either the board compliance committee or an executive position as compliance and risk officer. Governance, risk management, and compliance reporting (GRC) have evolved to mitigate the rising economic challenges. Specifically, compliance risk has increased due to the widening business complexity, need to reduce risk exposure, and mission to improve firm performance. Companies and their board of directors will have to give considerable attention to compliance risk or face consequences such as fines and public scrutiny.

Reputation Risk

Maintaining a good business reputation while meeting and exceeding expectations of corporate stakeholders from investors to creditors, suppliers, customers, employees, the environment, and society is a major challenge for many businesses. Social risks are growing increasingly more common and run a great risk to the financial and reputational standings of a company. All five EGSEE dimensions of sustainability performance are associated with business reputation, customer satisfaction, and the ethical workplace. The company's reputation and its related risk should be evaluated on and ongoing basis and any damages to the reputation must be minimized. The social risk theory suggests that every company faces an unavoidable reputational risk related to corporate social responsibility initiatives. Research by Christine Jacob shows that many companies have a better understanding of the importance of social risks and their impact on reputation, but they do not necessarily report it openly.[8] Most companies give importance to issues related directly to shareholders such as financial risks and those risks that are perceived as most influential.

---

[8] Jacob, C. 2012. "The Impact of Financial Crisis on Corporate Social Responsibility and Its Implications for Reputation Risk Management." *Journal of Management and Sustainability*, August 10, 2020. https://heinonline.org/HOL/Page?handle=hein.journals/jms2&id=491&collection=journals&index=

Financial Risk

Nonfinancial dimensions of sustainability performance, including ethical, social, governance, and environmental dimensions can affect financial performance. The financial risk of issuing materially misstated financial reports is detrimental to the overall sustainability of corporations. Further, sustainability reports are expected to be value-relevant to both external and internal users of such reports and free of material financial misstatements. Investors and other stakeholders including suppliers, customers, government, and society can have more transparent information about financial ESP and nonfinancial EESG sustainability performance, which enable them to make more informed decisions. Sustainability reporting improves internal management practices by enabling companies to establish better relationships with their investors, customers, suppliers, employees, regulators, and eventually society. When companies use sustainability reporting, this creates more incentives for management to refocus its goals, strategic decisions, and actions from a short-term to a long-term prospect.

Sustainability reporting can be used as a tool for a more effective risk management of identifying both opportunities and risks associated with operations. Thus, more transparent sustainability disclosures on financial ESP and nonfinancial EESG sustainability performance create opportunities to identify and correct operational inefficiencies, reputational, and financial risks that would improve economic performance. Best practices of sustainability suggest that companies that ignore their financial ESP and nonfinancial EESG sustainability performance issues and responsibilities would encounter the risk of: (1) not maintaining sustainability in the long term; (2) being subject to higher scrutiny and intervention by regulators; (3) losing their license to operate; (4) losing customer reputation and confidence in their products and services; (5) not being able to attract most qualified and talented human capital and workforce; (6) incurring a higher cost of capital both in debt and equity; (7) having less of an analyst following, which may affect their market valuation; (8) not attracting investors with long-term horizons; (9) encouraging managerial practices of not being sensitive or accountable for multi-dimension stakeholders; and (10) not setting an appropriate tone at the top by directors and executives in promoting ethical, accountable, socially, and environmentally responsible behavior and practices throughout the organization.

Cyber Security Risk

Destructive cyberattacks, such as the Sony Pictures incident, are considered the most damaging cyberattacks outside the norms of cyber practices and can be detrimental to sustainability of public companies. Technological advancements have turned cyber security into becoming the top agenda of the board of directors and executives for every company. While the United States has accused the government of North Korea for the Sony cyberattack, the group that identifies itself as the Guardians of Peace has claimed responsibility for the attack.

The U.S. government is considering a "proportional response" against those who are responsible for the Sony cyberattack.[9] Cyber hacking can be detected and prevented by using effective and efficient cyber security procedures driven by information security management system (ISMS). Use of this family of standards will help organizations to manage the security of assets such as financial information, intellectual property, employee details, or information entrusted to the entities by third parties.[10] ISMS is a systematic approach to managing sensitive company information so that it remains protected. Furthermore, it helps identify the risks to important information and put the appropriate controls in place to reduce the risk. It includes people, processes, and IT systems by applying a risk management process. This standard is available to help any size organization, whether it is small, medium, or large businesses in any sector.

---

[9] Banker, P. 2014. "US weighs Response to Sony Cyberattack, with North Korea Confrontation Possible." *New York Times*, December 18. http://nytimes .com/2014/12/19/world/asia/north-korea-confrontation-possible-in-response-to-sony-cyberattack.html?_r=0

[10] ISO 27001 – Information security management. http://iso.org/iso/home/standards/management-standards/iso27001.htm

COVID-19 Pandemic Risk

The COVID -19 pandemic risk is defined as the possibility that an event such as fraudulent financial information at the company level could trigger severe instability or collapse in an entire industry or economy or an even such as the COVID-19 pandemic could cause global devastation and crisis. This systemic risk has a potential to destabilize global capital markets, financial systems, and the broader economy. The COVID-19 pandemic risks need to be assessed and managed because these risks could have disruptive and significant impacts on asset valuations, global financial markets, and economic stability. The overwhelming global responses and stimulate financial packages could put significant financial burden on many countries and threaten their sustainability.

The pandemic risk is an important subject to be taken into consideration during and in the aftermath of the COVID-19 pandemic. Since the rapid spread of Coronavirus in early 2020, companies all around the world have seen a slowdown in operations, downsizing, and other negative impacts. Indeed, many businesses terribly struggled, ending up in discontinuance and bankruptcy within a short period of time. Therefore, it is crucial that companies scrutinize pandemic risk when making strategic decisions and take appropriate actions to protect their shareholders and stakeholders during pandemics like COVID-19.

There are multiple EESG factors to consider regarding pandemic risks, such as board oversight of risk management, critical incident and systemic risk management, human capital issues, business model resilience, supply chain resilience, executive compensation, dividend payouts and stock buybacks, customer welfare and impact on communities, shareholder engagement, and critical ESG disclosures. The first EESG factor discussed here is the board oversight of risk management. In the light of crisis like COVID-19, any firm should prepare to address the concerns of their investors, employees, customers, and other stakeholders. This requires boards of the companies to fully understand what risks are faced and what concerns need to be addressed. To accomplish such a goal, regular communication between directors and management about operations and stakeholder-related issues is a necessity. The boards should also reassess both short-term and long-term strategic plans to maintain business continuity with an emphasis on issues such as capital allocation, credits, public relations, and new regulations compliance.

There are also controversies about whether the board of directors should establish a separate Risk Oversight Committee in response to the COVID-19 pandemic. Many believe the best way to manage various types of risks is to divide such responsibility among the different committees in the boards such as Audit Committee, Nominating and Governance Committee, and Compensation Committee. Furthermore, adding a Special Oversight Committee may create problems related to time constraints and board structure (especially for companies with a small number of directors). However, facing special situations like pandemics, boards with a separate Risk Committee may be presented with opportunities to gain special insights into such unique circumstances. This committee can meet on short notice to discuss issues and actions related to the crisis and improve the quality of the corporate oversight.

The second factor to consider is critical incident. Pandemics like COVID-19 shows the vulnerability of companies and industries to incidents that are less likely to happen but leave severe impacts. These critical events have detrimental effects on operating cash flow, credit ratings, capital access, supply chain, customer relationship, employee well-being, and corporation reputation. Therefore, it is important for companies to implement more dynamic and comprehensive risk management to maintain business continuity. Plus, regarding the shift to virtual platform during the pandemic, companies should be more cautious about collecting, storing, and sharing sensitive data on their systems to avoid threats from hackers and other cybersecurity threats.

Another important EESG factor is human capital issues such as employee well-being, health, and safety. Effective implementation of safety measurements and good communication are beneficial during pandemics. For example, dealing with COVID-19 pandemic, companies should implement safety protocols and effectively communicate with employees to limit the spread of virus. In addition, firms should provide employees with sufficient and protective gears, sick pay, financial assistance, flexibility at work, and technological assistance for working from home. Amid the pandemic, it is common to see layoffs and salary reductions, in these cases companies need to ensure their employees are given notice in advance and receive necessary financial assistance while maintaining law compliance. Regarding the retained workforce, corporations should evaluate their employees' competence to meet demands after the pandemic is under control.

It is also important to consider the resilience of business model and supply chain. As the society and industries evolve quickly during crisis, business models need to be more adaptable to changes and companies should have the appropriate strategies under different scenarios. Significant instances can be observed during COVID-19 pandemic when travel industries suffer terribly due to travel restrictions while medical and sanitizing suppliers see a surge in demand. Such uncertainty encourages firms to become more flexible in preparation for future contingency. During the pandemic, supply chain also suffers from many problems, such as shortage of medical supplies, lack of infrastructure, and panic buying behaviors. Therefore, global companies need to determine and improve the weaknesses of the supply chains to deal with any future disruptions.

Other relevant EESG factors include executive compensation, dividend payouts, and stock buybacks. It is advisable for companies to update their executive compensation plans to reflect economic difficulties. Executive compensation limits can be found in the Coronavirus Aid, Relief, and Economic Security Act (the "CARES Act"). Similarly, the CARES Act limits the amount of dividend payouts and stock buybacks for businesses participating in the federal assistance program. In fact, a lot of companies had to avoid paying dividends and repurchasing stocks to maintain liquidity. As a lesson for the future, firms should try to optimize their capital allocation to cope with uncertainties of the economy during the pandemic.

Consumer welfare and impact on local communities should also be of concern. During the pandemic, there are a few industries operating at the frontline including health care providers, transportation, and shipping services, as well as necessities providers like grocery chains and banks. These businesses greatly facilitate in the fight against pandemic by protecting health of citizens while meeting their basic needs during the quarantine. However, these companies need to handle the risk of overexploiting their workforce and resources, especially at peak times. Moreover, a lot of big corporations can assist in the relief efforts through donations and intellectual contributions. For firms that are not operating at the frontline, it is necessary to adjust their products, infrastructure, resources, and services to meet special needs from customers during these unique circumstances. More importantly, the way a corporation makes an impact on and contributions to the communities may serve as a reference for future evaluations in terms of social and reputational aspects.

The next EESG factor addresses the shareholder engagement among firms. Investors and other stakeholders need a lot of reassurance during pandemic as they become much more anxious about their investments during a time of crisis. Therefore, companies need to engage shareholders with clear and regular communication about operations status and approach to multiple issues. In response to the COVID-19 pandemic the board of directors and management should focus on short-term strategic plans to ensure business continuity and survival as well as long-term sustainable strategic plans to ensure long-term well-being and value creation for all stakeholders. The board of directors and management should effectively communicate with their shareholders and other stakeholders about the impacts of the pandemic on the firms' short-term, medium-term, and long-term strategies, as well as their approach in addressing significant EESG issues.

Finally, nonfinancial EESG sustainability performance disclosures remain an increasingly important topic among the business organizations. Regarding the severe impacts of the pandemic like COVID-19, companies are expected to have extensive disclosures about the suffering and actions taken. In the aftermath of the COVID-19 pandemic, business organizations will be able to evaluate their weaknesses and vulnerabilities in a short-term while shareholders become more concerned about long-term sustainability and resilience of businesses, which can lead to the need for additional EESG disclosures. More importantly, corporations should take lessons from the pandemic to form future policies and disclosures about EESG.

Litigation Risk

Litigation risks could arise in EESG reporting issues due to the framework in the disclosing of scenario analysis. When using scenario analysis to understand future business performance through a variety of potential climate-based scenarios, the disclosure of these results and analysis, or lack thereof, is what gives way to possible litigation issues. Risks could come from missed climate-based scenarios, or whether working papers, regarding scenario analysis and could be used to commence litigation. Inaccurate or misleading material information from these scenarios is also a big potential litigation risk. Investors such as shareholders and creditors are looking for transparent and efficient information that can be utilized for effective decision making. Information and disclosures of a company should include all material matters to help defer the risks of litigation resulting from inadequate reports and inappropriate assumptions. These risks stem from lack of preparation for future events such as the COVID-19 pandemic, giving rise to a potentially misleading set of financial statements.

Climate Risk

The global climate change is real and the expected transitions to a net-zero carbon economy could put more pressures on the economic sustainability of many countries. Climate risks include the detrimental effects of: (1) the physical risk of rising temperatures about 1.8 F degree since the mid-20th century; (2) the threat of global greenhouse gas (GHG) emissions; and (3) natural disasters of catastrophic flooding, wildfires, storms, and droughts. The 2019 CDP survey reveals that 215 of the world's largest public companies could suffer about $1 trillion of climate-related risk in the next five years.[11] The climate risk can be assessed, managed, and its negative impacts be minimized if business organizations:

1. Acknowledge that climate change poses risks to their operational effectiveness, financial market stability, and financial sustainability.
2. Integrate climate change into their strategic planning and decision, corporate culture, and business environment.

---

[11] CDP. 2019. "World's Biggest Companies Face $1 Trillion in Climate Change Risks." June 4, 2019. Available at https://cdp.net/en/articles/media/worlds-biggest-companies-face-1-trillion-in-climate-change-risks

3. Explore the integration of climate risk into all aspects of business from operational to financial and supply chain.

4. Assess the adequacy and effectiveness of internal controls in responding to climate risks.

5. Disclose properly and transparently the climate risk to all stakeholders.

Sustainability Risk Assessment and Management

Identification of sustainability risks is the first step in the sustainability risk assessment and management. The Committee of Sponsoring Organizations (COSO) Enterprise Risk Management framework (ERM) should be used in assessing and managing sustainability risks.[12] All eight components of the COSO ERM framework should be assessed and managed including (1) internal environment of setting the tone of an organization in promoting sustainability factors of performance, risk, and disclosure; (2) objective setting of achieving short-, median-, and long-term sustainability; (3) risk identification of risk exposures relevant to potential sustainability issues; (4) risk assessment of determining risk root cause and sensitivity analyses of the drivers and pathways of organizational risks; (5) risk responses of addressing the drivers of sustainability risks; (6) control activities designed to manage sustainability risks; (7) information and communication of the organization's responses and efforts in assessing and managing sustainability risks and proper communication with all effected stakeholders; and (8) monitoring of ensuring that an organization in achieving its sustainability objectives, managing related sustainability risks, and monitoring and evaluating its sustainability activities.[13]

The COSO EMR framework also suggests several tips for raising sustainability awareness in the organization including: (1) getting leadership involved by embedding sustainability into corporate culture and

---

[12] Committee of Sponsoring Organizations of the Treadway Commission (COSO). 2013. "Demystifying Sustainability Risk." May 2013. Available at https://coso.org/documents/COSO-ERM%20Demystifying%20Sustainability%20Risk_Full%20WEB.pcf

[13] Ibid.

business environment and getting leadership (the board of directors, executives) involved in sustainability strategic planning; (2) engaging stakeholders (investors, employees, suppliers, customers) in sustainability initiatives and activities; (3) integrating sustainability into the business strategies; (4) identifying, assessing, and managing material sustainability risks; (5) looking for sustainability achievements and quick wins; (6) properly communicating sustainability good, bad and ugly stories; (7) selecting appropriate measurement tools by using balanced scorecards.[14]

Conclusion

Maintaining sustainability requires an intricate understanding of both performance and risks and their relationship and integration into the corporate culture as well as all levels of management strategies, decisions, and actions. There are several risks that are associated with both financial ESP and nonfinancial EESG business sustainability performance and include the following: strategic, operations, compliance, financial, and reputation, the COVID-19 pandemic, cybersecurity, climate change, and litigation risks. These risks have the potential to adversely impact business operations and finances, destabilize capital markets, and could lead to serious negative consequences for these business organizations and even the broader economy where they operate. Proper assessment, management, and disclosure of those risks are becoming increasingly important and play an effective role in achieving both financial ESP and nonfinancial EESG sustainability performance in creating shared value for all stakeholders.

Takeaways

1. More than 1,300 institutional investors worldwide, representing $59 trillion in assets under management, have signed on to the UN Principles of Responsible Investing, which seek to integrate sustainability factors of performance and risk into investment objectives.

---

[14] Ibid.

2. Use of Enterprise Risk Management (ERM) can turn sustainability challenges and risk into sustainability opportunities and performance.
3. Move toward sustainability reporting and risk assessment underscores the importance of an adequate ERM in improving the effectiveness of both financial ESP and nonfinancial EESG sustainability performance.
4. Use ISO 31000: Risk Management—Principles and Guidelines in 2009 that provides principles and guidelines on risk management.
5. Identify and assess all several EESG-related risks discussed in this chapter.
6. Properly disclose assessment and management sustainability risks and their possible impacts on operational and financial performance.

CHAPTER 4

Sustainability Disclosure Factor

Executive Summary

Prior chapters present sustainability performance and risk factors. Sustainability disclosure is another important factor of business sustainability. Sustainability disclosure provides financial information on economic sustainability performance (ESP) and nonfinancial on environmental, ethical, social, and governance (EESG) sustainability performance. As of now, disclosure of ESP information is mandatory in many countries whereas EESG information is typically disclosed on a voluntary basis except for large European companies starting in 2017, Hong Kong listed companies in 2016, and public companies in some other countries. Voluntary disclosure is considered as any financial and nonfinancial information disclosed by management beyond mandatory financial reports consisting of strategic information (product, competition, customers), financial information (management earnings forecast, stock price), and nonfinancial EESG information. This chapter presents the sustainability disclosure factor.

Introduction

Global public companies today face the challenges of adapting proper sustainability strategies and practices to effectively respond to social, ethical, environmental, and governance issues while creating sustainable financial performance and value for their shareholders. Business sustainability has recently evolved from the focus on short-term financial economic performance and fulfillment of corporate social responsibility (CSR) to the achievement of long-term financial economic sustainability performance (ESP) and nonfinancial environmental, ethical, social, and governance EESG sustainability performance in creating shared value for all stakeholders. Many public companies in Europe and Asia are now required to disclose their nonfinancial EESG sustainability performance information. It is expected that public companies in other countries follow the suite in requiring disclosure of sustainability information. This chapter presents both mandatory and voluntary disclosure of sustainability information.

Corporate Disclosure

Corporate disclosures, both mandatory on ESP information and voluntary on EESG sustainability performance information, are vital to the financial markets and value-relevant to investors and other stakeholders. The type and extent of voluntary disclosures have recently received considerable attention as many firms worldwide disclose information on various environmental, ethical, social, and governance (EESG) dimensions of their sustainability performance. Corporate disclosure, either mandatory on ESP or voluntary on EESG, is intended to provide investors and other stakeholders with relevant, useful, transparent, and reliable information in making sound investment decisions and thus it is the backbone of the financial markets. Public companies have disclosed a set of financial statements to their shareholders under the corporate mandatory disclosure regime and they also communicate with shareholders and other stakeholders through a variety of channels including corporate voluntary disclosures of EESG information. Anecdotal evidence suggests that investors value meaningful and reliable voluntary disclosures and use them in making investment decisions and to utilize mandatory disclosures to verify voluntary disclosures.[1] Thus, given the limited resources, management may trade-off the relative costs of mandatory and voluntary disclosures and may adjust the level of voluntary disclosure according to the level of mandatory disclosure in providing relevant, useful, and reliable financial ESP and nonfinancial EESG information.

---

[1] Ernst and Young (EY). 2014. "Disclosure Effectiveness: What Investors, Company Executives and other Stakeholders are Saying." Available at https://eyjapan.jp/library/issue/us/gaap-weekly-update/pdf/GAAP-2014-11-25-03.pdf

It is possible that management be more inclined to release mandatory ESP disclosures than disclosing voluntary EESG information or act in a similar or opposite direction regarding disclosing EESG information. Arguably, investors may view mandatory ESP information and voluntary EESG information as complementary or contradictory. Voluntary EESG disclosures represent management discretion of what information to disclose and what extent to disclose such information. Public companies are required to disclose mandatory financial information whereas they may choose to disclose the type and extent of nonfinancial EESG disclosures in striking a right balance between enhancing long-term shareholder value and creating shared value for all stakeholders while meeting the short-term expectations of investors. Sustainability EESG disclosures are largely not mandated, and managers may opportunistically determine their disclosure strategies.

Voluntary Sustainability Disclosures

Voluntary disclosure often takes the form of corporate responsibility reports and responses to surveys or data requests and is influenced by management discretion and guidelines used in disclosing nonfinancial EESG. The fourth generation (G4) of GRI's Guidelines covers economic, governance, social, and environmental performance with ethics component integrated into other dimensions of sustainability and the GRI globally accepted sustainability standards emphasize on both financial ESP and nonfinancial EESG sustainability performance. The GRI reporting process enables organizations to self-declare sustainability information based on one of three application levels (A, B, or C) depending on the extent of the information provided. The GRI initially focused on a triple-bottom line of economic, social, and environmental performance with version 3.1 (G3) of its sustainability framework. However, in 2011 the GRI developed version 4.1 or the fourth generation (G4) of guidelines, which covers economic, governance, social, and environmental performance and in 2016 established globally accepted sustainability standards (GASS) which focus on both financial and nonfinancial sustainability disclosures.

In September 2014, The European Commission adopted by the Council of the Directive on disclosure of nonfinancial sustainability information for more than 6,000 companies for their financial year 2017.[2] The directive provides nonbinding guidelines in facilitating the disclosure of nonfinancial environmental, social, anticorruption, and diversity information by large public companies. The directive also provides large companies with significant flexibility to disclose nonfinancial information either as a separate report or an integrated report along with financial information. The primary objectives of the directive are to: (1) increase transparency in sustainability reporting; (2) increase sustainability performance on social and environmental matters; and (3) contribute effectively to long-term economic growth and employment. Affected companies should report their:[3]

- Environmental performance
- Social and employee-related materials
- Human rights policies
- Anticorruption and bribery issues
- Diversity on the board of directors

Arguments about the detrimental effects of conventional financial reporting focusing only on economic performance are mounting as investors have shown interest in both financial and nonfinancial disclosures. While financial information may have a short-term impact on market efficiency and thus require interim trading updates, in the long-term it will lead to substantial pressures on management from the market to meet short-term targets. There are basically two detrimental effects of conventional financial reporting: (1) it encourages short-termism of achieving short-term financial performance; and (2) it compromises the quality of financial reporting by enabling management to engage in earnings management. Short-termism is defined as a phenomenon that leads managerial decisions and actions disproportionally toward achieving short-term

---

[2] European Commission. 2014. "Disclosure of Non-Financial Information: Europe's Largest Companies to be more Transparent on Social and Environmental issues." September 29, 2014. Available at http://ec.europa.eu/internal_market/accounting/non-financial_reporting/index_en.htm
[3] Ibid.

earnings targets at the expense of sustainable performance. Conventional financial reporting encourages management to focus on short-term performance and the goal of meeting or exceeding short-term targets or analysts' forecast estimates. Such an impact on management behavior prevents management from directing its resources toward sustainable and enduring plans, activities, and EGSEE sustainability performance. Uncertainty about the future, including government policies, regulations, markets, and other unforeseeable factors, such as the 2020 COVID-19 pandemic, drive managerial planning to short-term considerations rather than long-term sustainable performance.

Consequences of short-term considerations (short-termism) are a divergence of resources from contributing to economic growth and ineffective misallocation of resources in several ways, including: (1) sacrificing, delaying, or decreasing discretionary spending on long-term investments or projects to achieve short-term financial targets that meet financial market expectations; (2) gearing management's time and efforts toward meeting expectations of short-term results rather than focusing on activities that add sustainable value to the company; (3) encouraging earnings management by either deferring costs or shifting revenues; (4) tying excessive executive compensation to the achievement of short-term financial targets at the expense of sustainable economic value creation; (5) higher risk premiums resultant from frequent trading done by speculators who target short-term movement in stock prices; (6) incurring expenses by mutual funds because of overactive trading caused by focus on short-term considerations; and (7) delaying investment in sustainability initiatives. This short-termism practice undermines the sustainable economic performance of many companies by encouraging management to emphasize short-term financial performance with less or no focus on the sustainability of economic performance and its impacts on people, planet, and society measured in terms of EESG sustainability performance. Sustainability reporting, on the other hand, reduces pressures on management from the market to meet short-term targets and thus has potential to affect earnings management.

The European Commission has long promoted CSR and its integration into corporate strategic decisions by defining CSR as "a concept whereby companies integrate social and environmental concerns in their business."[4] This definition of CSR suggests companies take social actions above and beyond their mandatory requirements toward society and environment. Business sustainability with a keen focus on CSR can "bring benefits in terms of risk management, cost savings, access to capital, customer relationships, human resource management, and innovation capacity."[5] Thus, disclosure of such information promotes interaction with all stakeholders on important nonfinancial ESG sustainability performance. Disclosure of nonfinancial ESG sustainability performance demonstrates companies' commitment and move toward achieving the European Union's treaty objectives of "the Europe 2020 strategy for smart, sustainable, and inclusive growth, including the 75 percent employment target."[6] It also facilitates engagement with stakeholders regarding sustainable growth and risks in building trust in the company and shareholders regarding allocation capital and achievement of long-term investment goals.

Global and national stock exchanges have promoted sustainability performance reporting by adopting laws, regulations, and listing standards that specifically mandate sustainability reporting. In recent years, many countries including Australia, Austria, Canada, Denmark, France, Germany, Malaysia, Netherlands, Sweden, Hong Kong, and the United Kingdom have adopted stand-alone ESP and ESG sustainability performance reports.[7] It is expected that regulators in other countries follow suit, moving toward mandatory sustainability performance reporting. Stock exchanges worldwide either require or recommend that their listed companies report sustainability information (e.g., Singapore Stock Exchange, 2011; Toronto Stock Exchange, 2014 (TSX, 2014); Hong Kong Stock Exchange, 2015 (HKEx, 2015)), and more than 6,000 European companies will be required to disclose their nonfinancial ESG sustainability

---

[4] European Commission (EUC). 2011. Communication from the Commission to the European Parliament, The Council, the European Economic and Social Committee and the Committee of the Regions, Brussels, October 25, 2011, COM(2011) 681 final.

[5] Ibid.

[6] Ibid.

[7] Rezaee (2015).

Table 4.1 Sustainability professional organizations

	Organization / Standard	Year Implemented	Location	Mission
CDP	Formerly Carbon Disclosure Project (now formally known by its acronym)	2000	London, United Kingdom	To conduct studies relevant to distinct areas: carbon footprint; water usage; deforestation; supply chain as well as releasing ratings based on survey responses.
CDSB	Climate Disclosure Standards Board	2007	London, United Kingdom	Promote disclosure regulations and guidelines and make recommendations.
GRI	Global Reporting Initiative	1997	Amsterdam, Netherlands	To establish ESG sustainability standards for external reporting.
IIRC	International Integrated Reporting Council	2010	London, United Kingdom	Promote its integrated sustainability reporting in six-capital approach.
SASB	Sustainability Accounting Standards Board	2011	San Francisco, Calif.	Establish ESG sustainability standards to be integrated into financial reporting.
SDG	United Nations Global Compact—Sustainable Development Goals	2015	United Nations (global)	Issue the 17 SDGs to be used by organizations worldwide.

performance and diversity information for their financial year 2017.[8] Table 4.1 presents organizations that provide guidelines and standards for promoting and practicing sustainability.

---

[8] Ibid.

Mandatory Sustainability Disclosure

In the past several decades, growing concerns regarding financial scandals (e.g., Swissair, Enron, WorldCom, Adelphia, Palmarat, Satyam, Bear Stearns, Lehman Brothers, Wirecard among others), the environmental impact, corporate social responsibility, governance, and ethical behavior of corporations have encouraged policymakers and regulators to address these concerns by establishing laws and regulations to minimize their negative impacts. One example in the United States is the passage of the Sarbanes-Oxley Act (SOX) of 2002 to combat financial statement fraud and prevent further occurrences of financial scandals by improving corporate governance measures and financial reporting and audit processes.[9] SOX (2002) and related Securities and Exchange Commission (SEC) regulations also require public companies in the United States to establish and maintain an effective internal control over financial reporting to combat fraud and irregularities in reporting related to governmental laws and SEC regulations. The SEC in the past several decades has issued numerous regulations for disclosure of environmental liabilities including Releases Number 5170 in 1971, Number 5386 in 1973, the climate change interpretive guidance in 2010, and conflict minerals rules in 2012.[10]

In recent years, many countries including Australia, Austria, Canada, Denmark, France, Germany, Malaysia, Netherlands, Sweden, Hong Kong, and the United Kingdom have adopted mandatory reporting on financial economic sustainability performance (ESP) and nonfinancial EESG sustainability performance.[11] It is expected that regulators in other countries follow suit, moving toward mandatory sustainability performance reporting and assurance. Stock exchanges worldwide either require or recommend that their listed companies report sustainability information (e.g., Singapore Stock Exchange 2011; Toronto Stock Exchange 2014;

---

[9] Sarbanes–Oxley Act 2002, Pub. L. 107-204, enacted July 30, 2002, adding 15 U.S.C. § 7201 *et seq.* and adding and am sending other provisions of the United States Code, as explained in the notes accompanying 15 U.S.C. §7201, hereinafter in this portfolio the "Sarbanes-Oxley Act" or "SOX."

[10] Rezaee (2015).

[11] Rezaee, Z. 2015. *Business Sustainability: Performance, Compliance, Accountability and Integrated Reporting.* Greenleaf Publishing Limited, Sheffield, UK.

Hong Kong Stock Exchange 2015), and more than 6,000 European companies are required to disclose their nonfinancial ESEG sustainability performance and diversity information for their financial year 2017 and onward.[12]

The Hong Kong Exchange has recently announced that an integrated sustainability and corporate governance report will be required for Hong Kong listed companies starting 2015.[13] This guide requires environmental, social, and governance. The Exchange encourages an issuer to identify and disclose additional ESG issues and KPIs that are relevant to its business. An issuer may adopt a higher level of ESG reporting based on international guidance standards such as IIRC and GRI. There are four ESG subject areas: Workplace Quality, Environmental Protection, Operating Practices, and Community Involvement. It is important to engage stakeholders periodically to identify material aspects and KPIs and understand their views. In compliance with these standards:

1. An issuer may disclose the ESG information in its annual report regarding the same period covered in the annual report, or in a separate report, in print or on its website.
2. Issuers may consider offering assurance on the ESG report.

Department of Labor (DOL) Proposed ESG Rule

Environmental, social, and governance (ESG) standards are under heightened scrutiny and the underlying themes and traditions are being challenged by today's society. The Department of Labor (DOL) has released proposed rules on ESG that would prohibit a retirement plan fiduciary from making any investment, or choosing an investment fund, based

---

[12] European Commission. 2014. "Disclosure of non-financial information: Europe information: Europe Council, the European Economic and Social, Environmental Issues." Available online at http://ec.europa.eu/internal_market/accounting/non-financial_reporting/index_en.htm, (accessed on March 29, 2016).

[13] Hong Kong Stock Exchange (HKEx). January 13, 2015. "Appendix 27 Environmental, Social and Governance Reporting Guide." Retrieved July 28, 2015, from http://hkex.com.hk/eng/rulesreg/listrules/mbrules/documents/appendix_27.pdf

on the consideration of an environmental, societal, or governmental factor unless that factor independently represents a material economic investment consideration under generally accepted investment theories or serves as a tiebreaker in what the DOL characterizes as the rare case of economically equivalent investments.[14] Therefore, the plan fiduciaries will be required to compare the investments on factors such as liquidity and diversification. Specific documentation would be required for the tiebreaker justification and for the selection and monitoring of an investment alternative in a 401(k) plan that includes ESG in its mandate or fund name.

Most significantly, the proposed rules would prohibit a 401(k) plan from providing a qualified default investment alternative ("QDIA") with an ESG component, no matter how small, even if that investment alternative satisfies the pecuniary factor requirements. At the same time, if implemented, the new rules may spur further demand for comparable, decision-useful ESG data to help satisfy the burden imposed by the DOL to justify the inclusion of ESG factors in private-sector retirement plans. The rules may also accelerate the work being done in business schools, academia, investment houses, and sophisticated finance and valuation venues to measure EESG's impact and ensure that generally accepted investment theories do not have value relevant EESG blind spots.[15]

Sustainability Disclosures

Disclosure of sustainability financial ESP and nonfinancial EESG information can be reflected in the sustainability reports. Reliability, objectivity, and creditability of sustainability reports can be improved by obtaining sustainability assurance statements on sustainability reports. Sustainability reports can also achieve general acceptance and recognition by being evaluated and ranked by professional organizations. This

---

[14] Lipton and Wachtell. 2020. "DOL Proposes New Rules Regulating ESG Investments." Available at: https://corpgov.law.harvard.edu/2020/07/07/dol-proposes-new-rules-regulating-esg-investments/

[15] Ibid.

section presents sustainability reporting, assurance, ranking/index, and best practices.

Sustainability Reporting

There has been global progress in sustainability performance, reporting, and assurance in the past decade in response to the 2007–2009 Global Financial Crisis that has caused breakdowns in corporate governance, business sustainability, the ethical practices of corporations, and the 2020 COVID-19 pandemic and social unrest. Business organizations worldwide now recognize the importance of business sustainability in creating shared value for all stakeholders including shareholders in the aftermath of the 2020 COVID-19 pandemic. Sustainability reporting is the process of disclosing information relevant to both financial ESP and nonfinancial EESG sustainability performance information and sustainability assurance lends more credibility to sustainability reports. More than 15,000 business organizations worldwide are now issuing sustainability reports on the various dimensions of their sustainability performance.[16] About 20 percent of the S&P 500 companies produced nonfinancial EESG sustainability reports in 2011 whereas in 2012 more than 53 percent, about 72 percent in 2013, 86 percent in 2018, and more than 90 percent in 2019.[17] This steady growth in the number of public companies publishing sustainability reports is expected to continue.

Sustainability reporting is the process of measuring, classifying, and recognizing financial ESP and nonfinancial EESG sustainability performance and disclosing such information to all stakeholders. Investors and other external stakeholders including suppliers, customers, governments, society, and the environment can now have more transparent information about companies' commitment to sustainability. Sustainability reporting can be used by management to improve managerial strategic

---

[16] Rezaee, Z. 2016. "Business Sustainability Research: A Theoretical and Integrated Perspective." *Journal of Accounting literature* 36, pp. 48–64.

[17] Governance and Accountability Institute, INC. (G&A) 2020. 2020 Flash Report S&P 500. Available at https://ga-institute.com/research-reports/flash-reports/2020-sp-500-flash-report.html

decisions by integrating sustainability into the business environment, corporate culture, and supply chain management. Sustainability performance reporting and assurance can provide management and external stakeholders with improved confidence in the credibility and trustworthiness of sustainability information. Recently, more than 15,000 public companies worldwide are issuing sustainability reports on a voluntary basis on the various dimensions of sustainability performance. In May 2013, the GRI released its G4 Guidelines promoting sustainability reporting as a standard practice of disclosing sustainability performance dimensions relevant to companies and their stakeholders.[18] Now in 2020 the GRI has modified standards to reflect the changing economy and results from the COVID-19 pandemic.

The International Integrated Reporting Council (IIRC) suggests processes for making a comprehensive sustainability reports framework that merges financial ESP and nonfinancial EESG sustainability performance information into an "integrated" format that is relevant to all corporate stakeholders.[19] The 2020 revision for the IIRC welcomes the identifying metrics that support effective and long-term sustainability value creation and shows the universal need for financial and nonfinancial EESG standards. The Sustainability Accounting Standards Board (SASB) establishes sustainability accounting standards based on the U.S. Securities and Exchange Commission's (SEC) reporting, which mandates material disclosures for 88 industries in 10 sectors as part of mandatory filings with the SEC.[20] Several global professional organizations including the Global Reporting Initiative (GRI), the International Integrated Reporting

---

[18] Global Reporting Initiative (GRI). 2013. "G4 Sustainability Reporting Guidelines." May 2013, Available at https://globalreporting.org/Pages/default.aspx (accessed on August 10, 2017).

[19] International Integrated Reporting Committee (IIRC). 2014. "Integrated Reporting Committee (IRC) of South Africa. Preparing an Integrated Report a Starter's Guide." Available at: http://integratedreporting.org/resource/irc-of-south-africa-preparing-an-integrated-report/ (accessed on August 10, 2017).

[20] Sustainability Accounting Standards Board (SASB). 2013. "Conceptual Framework of Sustainability Accounting Standard Board." October 2013, Available at http://sasb.org/wp-content/uploads/2013/10/SASB-Conceptual-Framework-Final-Formatted-10-22-13.pdf (accessed on August 10, 2017).

Council (IIRC), and the Sustainability Accounting Standards Board (SASB) have promoted integrated sustainability reporting and assurance in the past decade. Global accounting standard-setters such as the International Accounting Standards Board (IASB) and the Financial Accounting Standards Board (FASB) are currently considering whether and how to establish accounting guidelines for the proper recognition and disclosure of all five dimensions of sustainability performance information.

Sustainability Assurance

Audits of financial statements and internal control over financial reporting (ICFR) have played a significant role in financial markets by lending more credibility and reliability to the financial information used by investors. The reliability and credibility of sustainability reports can be enhanced by providing assurance on such reports. However, the 2017 survey conducted by Ernst & Young (EY) indicates that: (1) investors are increasingly considering the important role that nonfinancial EESG sustainability dimensions play in their investment decision making; (2) management should present annual long-term board reviews of sustainability strategies; (3) a majority of surveyed companies have not considered environmental and social issues, their related risks, and the opportunities they present as core to their business; (4) generating sustainable financial ESP returns over time requires a sharper focus on nonfinancial EESG sustainability performance; and (5) nonfinancial EESG issues have a real and quantifiable impact on financial ESP sustainability over the long term.[21]

The SASB, in its 2013 Conceptual Framework for Sustainability, suggests that sustainability performance disclosures be made as a complete set in the Managements Discussion and Analysis of Financial Condition and Results of Operations (MD&A) section of Form 10-K, in a subsection titled "Sustainability Accounting Standard Disclosures" filed with the SEC and disseminated to shareholders. The IFAC released its revised

---

[21] Ernst & Young (EY). 2017. "Is your Non-Financial Performance Revealing the True Value of Your Business to Investors?" Available at: http://ey.com/gl/en/services/assurance/climate-change-and-sustainability-services/ey-nonfinancial-performance-may-influence-investors (accessed August 1, 2017).

"International Standard on Assurance Engagements Other Than Audits or Reviews of Historical Financial Information," 3000 (ISAE 3000). Specifically, ISAE 3410 deals with assurance engagements for an organization reporting greenhouse gas (GHG) statements. Alternatively, GRI can examine the content of declared sustainability reports and express an opinion on the extent of compliance with GRI guidelines, but not the quality and/or reliability of disclosed sustainability information. Unlike audit reports on financial statements, assurance reports on sustainability information are neither standardized nor regulated or licensed.

The American Institute of Certified Public Accountants (AICPA) has released sustainability attestation and materiality guides to assist practitioners in providing assurance statements on sustainability reports.[22] Sustainability assurance is not currently regulated in many countries; different types of entities provide assurance services using different scopes, methodologies, and assurance statements. In August 2019, the AICPA released a discussion paper on materiality considerations for sustainability-related attestation engagements, which provides assurance on material disclosures about an entity's sustainability efforts including an entity's internal control system, or instances of noncompliance.[23] The credibility of sustainability reports can be improved when they are accompanied by assurance statements from reputable assurance providers. The effectiveness of assurance reports can be achieved when assurance providers are provided by globally accepted and standardized assurance standards. Different levels of assurance be rendered by assurance providers on both, financial and nonfinancial, dimensions of sustainability performance based on the extent of assurance procedures performed and assurance evidence gathered. Specifically, the integrated sustainability assurance framework can be developed to

---

[22] American Institute of Certified Public Accounting (AICPA). 2017. New Sustainability Attestation Guide. July 27, 2017. Available at https://aicpa.org/press/pressreleases/2017/aicpa-issues-new-sustainability-attestation-guide.html

[23] American Institute of Certified Public Accounting (AICPA). 2019. "Discussion Paper: Materiality Considerations for Attestation Engagements Involving Aspects of Subject Matters that Cannot Be Quantitatively Measured." August 15, 2019. https://aicpa.org/content/dam/aicpa/interestareas/frc/assuranceadvisoryservices/downloadabledocuments/exposuredrafts/materiality-discussion-paper.pdf

provide sustainability assurance on all dimensions of sustainability performance reports can be classified into distinct sections or reports based on the degree of assurance and content as follows:

1. Positive and reasonable assurance on financial statements reflecting financial economic sustainability performance (ESP).
2. Positive and reasonable assurance on internal control over financial reporting (ICFR), as related to the economic dimension of sustainability performance.
3. Negative and limited assurance on sustainability reports pertaining to the nonfinancial environmental, ethical, social, and governance (EESG) dimensions of sustainability performance.

Business sustainability has extended the type and amount of both financial and nonfinancial information that business organizations provide to their stakeholders regarding their sustainability performance. As sustainability reporting is gaining acceptance as a common practice of corporate reporting, its credibility needs to be assured by assurance providers. Sustainability assurance can be public and for use by external stakeholders in lending more credibility to the published sustainability reports or private and internal users to give confidence and suggest improvements to the board and executives that the firm is doing the right thing in ensuring improvements in all financial and nonfinancial dimensions of sustainability performance. In providing assurance on sustainability reports, auditors should conduct their assurance services by performing the audit procedures summarized below:

1. Identify the externally designated and internally intended use and distribution of sustainability assurance reports.
2. Determine the reporting criteria and frameworks to be applied.
3. Define the objective and scope of information and processes to be assured including reasonable/positive assurance on financial ESP and limited/negative assurance on nonfinancial EESG dimensions of sustainability performance.
4. Identify auditing and assurance standards that are applicable in forming audit opinions on financial statements and ICFR as well as

assurance standards applicable to nonfinancial EESG sustainability performance reports.

5. Determine audit and assurance evidence that is supplied to and gathered by the assurance provider to support the provider's conclusion report.

6. Identify the expected form and content of the sustainability assurance report, the intended users, and the process for feedback to the reporting entity.

7. Provide independent assurance on both financial ESP and nonfinancial EESG sustainability performance reports.

Best Practices of Sustainability Performance Reporting and Assurance

Global trending toward business sustainability performance, risk, disclosure, reporting, and assurance encourages and ultimately rewards companies that focus on financial ESP and nonfinancial EESG dimensions of sustainability performance and disclose their sustainability performance in sustainability reports and assurance. Business organizations worldwide are now recognizing the importance of both ESP and EESG sustainability performance and the link between the bottom-line profitability and EESG sustainability. Justifications for EESG sustainability performance are social responsibility, moral obligation, maintaining a good reputation, environmental impacts, ensuring sustainability, licensing to operate, and creating shared value. In a shared value approach, corporations identify potential social and environmental issues of concern and integrate them into their strategic planning.

There are many factors of why a company should pay attention to nonfinancial EESG sustainability performance such as the pressure of the labor movement, development of moral values and social standards, the development of business education, and the change in public opinion about the role of business. Companies that are, or aspire to be, leaders in sustainability are challenged by rising public expectations, increasing innovation, continuous quality improvement, and heightened social and environmental problems. The businesses should fulfill the social responsibility and environmental initiatives due to the public image, consumer movements, government requirements, and investors' education, avoidance of environmental violations and obligations and tax benefits, better relations with stakeholders, employee satisfaction, a sense of pride, and an appropriate way to improve quality.

These high-profile and high-quality sustainability reporting and assurance organizations demonstrate that business sustainability can be successfully achieved when the following best practices being considered by companies worldwide:[24]

1. Promoting the move toward business substitutability by setting the tone at the top in engaging in sustainability initiatives. The board of directors as representatives of shareholders should consider the opportunities and challenges including risks offered by the global move toward sustainability and make sustainability issues at the top of board agenda. The board culture should be guided toward sustainability leadership and mindset of directors should be directed toward sustainability and sustainable strategic decisions to create shared value for all stakeholders and disclosure of sustainability performance achievements through sustainability reporting and assurance.

2. Executive commitments to sustainability performance and properly disclosing such performance. Corporate executives, particularly CEOs and CFOs, should have full commitment in achieving financial ESP and nonfinancial EESG dimensions of sustainability performance by moving away from greenwashing sustainability and moving toward sustainability strategic imperatives. Management should effectively disclose its sustainability performance achievement by issuing a high-quality sustainability reports and assurance as discussed in the previous sections.

3. Advancement of long-term sustainability investment strategies and performance. Individual investors as well as institutional investors should focus on long-term and sustainable investments rather than

short-termism market movements by integrating both ESP and EESG sustainability issues into their investment decisions.

4. Integration of sustainability performance reporting and assurance into corporate reporting and periodically issue sustainability reports accompanied with an assurance opinion.

Management should design, implement, and maintain proper sustainability processes and strategies that provide a common ground for the integration of sustainability to the corporate culture, business environment, strategic plans, and supply chain that consist of:

- Utilization of the stewardship theory with a keen focus on all capitals from strategic to financial, reputational, manufactured, social, environmental, and human in creating accountability and stewardship for all capitals and stakeholders.

- Integration of continuous improvement for both financial ESP and nonfinancial EESG sustainability performance into the business environment, corporate culture and investment analysis, supply chain management, and decision-making process.

- Establishment of tone at the top commitment by the company's board of directors and executives to effective and robust application of sustainability best practices in managing sustainability issues including environmental, human rights, and social issues across the operations and supply chains.

- Development of a long-term and sustainable relationship with all stakeholders. Collaboration among all stakeholders to enhance the effectiveness of implementing sustainability programs and development including strategies in creating shared value for all stakeholders is important in the development of such relationships.

- Engagement of all stakeholders to discuss the company's sustainability strategies and progress including environmental initiatives. It is vital to engage major suppliers to understand the effects of sustainability issues (e.g., human rights, societal, and environmental) on supply chains.

- Development of SCS strategies for the identification and selection of suppliers that focus on the achievement of their sustainability performance.
- Communication of the company's sustainability strategies, practices, and expectations to major suppliers and customers to mitigate risks and foster corporate values and culture. Failure to address sustainability issues (e.g., human rights, social, and environmental) can create the risk of litigation and damage to brand value and reputation, particularly as supply chains relevant to materials and labor have shifted to emerging markets.
- Integration of sustainability into all aspects of supply chain from purchasing and inbound logistics, production design, and manufacturing processes to marketing, distribution, outbound logistics, and customer services.
- Continuous assessment of the company's sustainability performance to monitor and improve supply chain sustainability and identify challenging areas that need further improvements.
- Link business sustainable performance to the corporate culture, company's strategy, and business model by focusing on the effects of sustainability issues (environmental, social, and human rights) on supply chains. Communicate the company's sustainability success stories to all stakeholders including shareholders and trading partners.
- Periodic disclosures of both financial and nonfinancial key performance indicators (KPIs) relevant to sustainability performance including disclosing information on greenhouse gas (GHG) emissions policies and procedures, as well as renewable energy resources and climate change that are designed to address the associated challenges, opportunities, and risks that affect business environment.

Sustainability Disclosure Metrics

Nonfinancial and financial metrics are benchmarks against which performance is evaluated and are often disclosed by a company when the performance or status of the business needs to be presented to investors. Some of these metrics are industry-specific, others relate to socioeconomic factors or macro-economic matters, and can vary across businesses and industries. Sustainability disclosure metrics tend to vary from business to business. The existing MD&A requirements are a strong guideline to follow; however, they may need adjustment for industry specifics or sustainability matters unrelated to finances.

The International Business Council (IBC) is a community of business leaders from all industries to address global relevant business issues and solutions. The IBC launched an initiative to identify a core set of material EESG metrics and recommended disclosures that could be reflected in the mainstream annual reports of companies on a consistent basis across industry sectors and countries.[25] These metrics and disclosures are organized into four pillars: Principles of governance, Planet, People, and Prosperity, which are aligned with the SDGs and principal EESG domains. The objective is to expand and amplify the work already completed by these initiatives while bringing mainstream problems to the report and reinventing by creating new standards. These core metrics consist of those well-established reporting requirements and expanded metrics are less well established in existing practice.

For years, investors have been advocating for public companies to disclose key EESG metrics in a manner that investors view as comparable, decision-useful and verifiable, whether in SEC filings (which many investors prefer due to the rigor associated with the SEC reporting process) or voluntary sustainability reports. All of the leading voluntary EESG frameworks, including those promulgated by the Sustainability Accounting Standards Board (SASB), the Global Reporting Initiative (GRI), and the Task Force on Climate-Related Financial Disclosures (TCFD), require disclosure of key EESG performance indicators and metrics. The SASB framework, in particular, was initially intended to be used in SEC filings and encouraged inclusion of ESG disclosure in the MD&A. Public

---

companies, however, typically include their EESG disclosures in voluntary sustainability reports as opposed to their Exchange Act filings for a variety of reasons, including concerns regarding: (i) whether EESG metrics are material to an understanding of the company's business and require disclosure; (ii) whether internal or external review of EESG metrics (e.g., by internal audit or disclosure teams) is adequate to make disclosure of such metrics "ready-for-prime-time" in SEC reports; (iii) the risk that inclusion of EESG metrics in Exchange Act reports would unnecessarily increase the financial and accounting burdens associated with periodic reporting; and (iv) heightened liability risk associated with disclosure of ESG metrics in materials filed under the Exchange Act or incorporated by reference in registration statements filed under the Securities Act of 1933 (notwithstanding the fact that statements in voluntary sustainability reports have under some circumstances already been cited as grounds for general anti-fraud claims).

The World Economic Forum, the International Business Council, and the Big Four accounting firms announced a new initiative, on September 22, 2020, to synthesize company sustainability reporting by attempting to establish a commonly accepted metrics for ESG sustainability reporting.[26] The WEF framework encourages disclosure on a "comply or explain" basis, with the proper explanations and acceptable reasons (e.g., materiality, confidentiality and legal constraints) for not disclosing to a particular disclosure metric. In this context, "materiality" is defined by the company based on its peculiarities and need not conform to any regulatory definition of the term. Reporting is encouraged and permitted through annual reports or proxy statements to ensure the board oversight and participation of sustainability disclosure. Companies are encouraged to continue the of use sustainability reports for any supplemental sustainability information. Sustainability matrices could be aligned with UNSDGs with in the frameworks of GRI, SASB, or other sustainability standard-setters and be consistent with four sustainability

---

[26] World Economic Forum (WEF). 2020. "White Paper. Measuring Stakeholder Capitalism Towards Common Metrics and Consistent Reporting of Sustainable Value Creation." September 22, 2020,. Available at the http://www3.weforum. org/docs/WEF_IBC_Measuring_Stakeholder_Capitalism_Report_2020.pdf

pillars of people, planet, prosperity, and principles of governance. There are 21 core metrics and 34 explained indicators that are quantitatively measurable and should be used in sustainability reporting.

Sustainability Ratings/Rankings

Sustainability factors of performance, risk, and disclosure can be evaluated for their effectiveness by professional organizations. Sustainability ratings are opinions of professionals, organizations, and individual experts on the relative standing of a company's sustainability factors and are intended to serve as a benchmark in assessing EESG sustainability performance. Sustainability rating industry lacks a clear definitional foundation due to the various agencies provided in the marketplace, therefore the term corporate sustainability systems (CSS) is used.[27] Further, the common characteristics of the CSSs are grouped into three typologies: indexes, rankings, and ratings.[28] The most current list of who the CSSs are and includes the following:

- CDP Climate, Water and Forests Scores
- SAM (Sustainable Asset Management)
- Sustainalytics
- MSCI ESG Ratings
- Bloomberg ESG Scores
- ISS-Oekom
- FTSE Russell ESG Ratings
- EcoVadis
- Refinitiv
- Vigeo-Eiris
- Standard Ethics

---

[27] Cash, D. 2020. "Sustainable Rating Agencies." In *Sustainable Financial Systems: The Global Context, Risks, and Responsibility,* ed. Ziolo, M. Routledge.

[28] Diez-Cañamero, B., T. Bishara, J.R. Otegi-Olaso, R. Minguez, and J. María Fernández. 2020. "Measurement of Corporate Social Responsibility: A Review of Corporate Sustainability Indexes, Rankings and Ratings." Sustainability 12, no.5, p. 2153.

Table 4.2 presents these sustainability rating agencies along with their mission and products. These agencies offer a variety of ranking services to the market. For example, Bloomberg, FTSE Russell, the CDP, and MSCI, offer sustainability rankings on the composite ESG and each component of environmental (E), social (S), and governance (G). Alternatively, Eco-Vadis offers specialize raking on supply chains sustainability. Refinitiv was initially created by Thomson Reuters and BlackRock in 2018—and subsequently was sold to the London Stock Exchange. Vigeo-Eiris, rating agency, was recently acquired by Moody's, whereas Morningstar acquired a 40 percent stake in Sustainalytics in 2017.

Conclusion

An ever-increasing interest in business sustainability in the past several decades has led to a growth in literature addressing the theoretical and practical implications of various dimensions of business sustainability. Business sustainability focuses on corporate activities including supply chains that generate long-term financial ESP of firm value maximization in creating shareholder value, as well as other activities that result in the achievement of nonfinancial EESG sustainability performance that protect the interests of all stakeholders. Human capital disclosure in the aftermath of the COVID-19 pandemic is gaining much attention as organizations are required to ensure safety, health, and well-being of their employees, suppliers, and customers. Investors want that their companies have proper policies and processes for employee's layoff, retention, health, and safety.

Business organizations worldwide are now recognizing the importance of sustainability factors of performance, disclosure, and risk. Business sustainability suggests that a firm must fulfill its stewardship responsibilities to all stakeholders including shareholders, creditors, the community, society, and the environment. Disclosure of ESP and EESG dimensions of sustainability performance while signaling management commitments to sustainability and establishing legitimacy with all constituencies poses a cost–benefit trade-off that has implications for investors and business organizations. In creating shared value for all stakeholders, management should identify potential financial, social, environmental, governance, and ethical

Table 4.2 Sustainability rating agencies

Rating Agency	Website/URL	
Institutional Shareholders Service (ISS)	http://issgovernance.com/files/ISSGovernanceQuickScoreTechDoc.pdf	Provides proxy voting and corporate governance services to institutional investors ISS Corporate Governance Quotient, 2002 Government Risk Indicator (GRID), 2010 ISS QuickScore since 2013
Governance Metrics International (GMI)	https://msci.com/esg-integration http://www3.gmiratings.com/	GMIRATINGS was formed in 2010 through the merger of three independent companies of the Corporate Library (1999), GovernanceMetrics International (2000), Audit Integrity (2002)
Standard & Poor's Corporate Governance Scores and Evaluations, 2004	http://leeds-faculty.colorado.edu/grossd/FNCE 4820 Fall 2013/S&P Corporate Governance Scores.pdf	Evaluating corporate governance effectiveness of S&P companies.
Corporate Library	http://bloomberg.com/research/stocks/private/snapshot.asp?privcapId=8081642 http://marketwired.com/press-release/The-Corporate- Library-and-GovernanceMetrics-International-Agree-to- Merge-1294553.htm	Established its Board Analyst rating service in December 2002
Investor Responsibility Research Center	http://irrcinstitute.org/	Its assessment tool, Benchmarked, includes more than 70 corporate governance data points.
Moody's Investors Service	https://moodys.com/	It provides corporate governance assessments as part of its corporate finance research product

Rating Agency	Website/URL	
CSR ratings in China	http://rksratings.com	The Rankins (RKS), the leading independent CSR-rating entity in China that provides annual CSR. The RKS CSR ratings are developed in China from the adapted guidelines and best practices used by international CSR rating agencies such as the Global Reporting Initiative GRI and the Sustainability Accounting Standards Board (SASB). The RKS CSR ratings are developed in China from the adapted guidelines and best practices used by international CSR rating agencies such as the Global Reporting Initiative GRI and the Sustainability Accounting Standards Board (SASB). The RKS CSR ratings are developed in China from the adapted guidelines and best practices used by international CSR rating agencies such as the Global Reporting Initiative GRI and the Sustainability Accounting Standards Board (SASB)ratings, with scores available from 2009
Institutional Shareholder Services, Inc. (ISS)	https://issgovernance.com/esg/rankings/environmental-social-qualityscore/	In February 2018, the proxy advisory firm, Institutional Shareholder Services, Inc. (ISS), launched the E&S QualityScore to provide investors a new metric to evaluate the ESG risk of their portfolio companies. The E&S QualityScore measures an issuer's disclosure on environmental and social issues, including sustainability governance, and identifies key disclosure omissions.
Glass Lewis	www.glasslewis.com/proxy-talk-sustainalytics-esg-profile-page-faq/	Glass Lewis is integrating review of an issuer's ESG disclosure into its proxy paper reports. Glass Lewis will incorporate Sustainalytics' (a third party provide of ESG data) research and ratings into its proxy research platform.

Table 4.2 (*Continued*)

Rating Agency	Website/URL	
Dow Jones Sustainability Index (DJSI)	https://eu.spindices.com/indices/equity/dow-jones-sustainability-world-index	DJSI provides benchmarks for investors in generating long-term shareholder value by integrating sustainability into their investment portfolios.
SDG index	www.sdgindex.org/reports/2018/	Assesses countries' distance to achieving the Sustainable Development Goals (SDGs) by providing detailed SDG to help identify implementation priorities for the SDGs.
United Nations Sustainability Development Goals (UNSDGs)	https://sustainabledevelopment.un.org/?menu=1300	several of UN SDGs such as SDG 9 (infrastructure, industrialization, and innovation), SDG 15 (life and land as a proxy for environmental attributes), and SDG 16 (peaceful and inclusive societies for sustainable development as a proxy for social attributes) are linked to sustainability reporting quality and quantity. Sustainability assurance quality and quantity statements are significantly associated with ESG scores and SDGs 9, 15, and 16 (proxies for social and environmental attributes).
ESG Score	www.esade.edu\itemsweb\biblioteca\bbdd\inbbdd\archivos\Thomson_Reuters_ESG_Scores.pdf	Thomson Reuters ESG Score measures company's ESG performance based on reported data in the public domain. The ESG sustainability disclosure component scores range from 0.1 for companies that disclose the minimum amount of ESG data to 100 for those that disclose every data variable collected by Thomson Reuters.

issues of concern and integrate them into its decision-making, strategic planning, and managerial processes including supply chain management.

Business sustainability indicates that the main objective function for business organizations is to create shareholder value by maximizing firm financial performance through continuous improvements of both financial ESP and nonfinancial EESG sustainability performance. The ESP and EESG sustainability performance dimensions are interrelated and complement/complete each other and thus they should be integrated into corporate culture, business environment and supply chain management. The focus of business sustainability should be on creating long-term and sustainable shared value for all stakeholders. This suggests that management realizes the importance of integrating sustainability into supply chain management and business operations. Companies should effectively and transparently communicate their business sustainability performance with all stakeholders by periodically releasing their sustainability reports. This suggests that management uses sustainability reporting to disclose its sustainability information to all stakeholders and to signal its good practices of business sustainability. Management should also assess and manage all six sustainability risks presented in this monograph in minimizing the risk. Investors should consider these risks in evaluating their existing investments and making decisions about future investments. The three sustainability factors of performance, disclosure, and risk are the cornerstone and foundation of business sustainability.

Takeaways

1. Integrated sustainability reports should reveal both financial ESP and nonfinancial EESG information of sustainability performance to all stakeholders.
2. Sustainability reporting should be aligned with the company's communication strategy and improve relationships with all key stakeholders.
3. Sustainability risks should be assessed and managed to minimize the negative impacts on financial performance.
4. Sustainability rankings can create a benchmark for the company's sustainability success.

About the Author

Zabihollah Rezaee (Zabi) is the Thompson-Hill Chair of Excellence, and Professor of Accountancy at the University of Memphis and has served a two-year term on the Standing Advisory Group (SAG) of the Public Company Accounting Oversight Board (PCAOB). He received his BS degree from the Iranian Institute of Advanced Accounting, his MBA from Tarleton State University in Texas, and his PhD from the University of Mississippi. Dr. Rezaee holds ten certifications, including Certified Public Accountant (CPA), Certified Fraud Examiner (CFE), Certified Management Accountant (CMA), Certified Internal Auditor (CIA), Certified Government Financial Manager (CGFM), Certified Sarbanes-Oxley Professional (CSOXP), Certified Corporate Governance Professional (CGOVP), Certified Governance Risk Compliance Professional (CGRCP), Chartered Global Management Accountant (CGMA) and Certified Risk Management Assurance (CRMA). He served as the 2012–2014 secretary of the Forensic & Investigative Accounting (FIA) Section of the American Accounting Association (AAA), served on Auditing Standards Committee of the Auditing Section of the AAA and is currently the editor of the *Journal of Forensic Accounting Research* (JFAR) one of the AAA journals. Dr. Rezaee was one of the finalists for the position of the Faculty Trustee at the University of Memphis in 2016 and the Ombudsperson position in 2017 and he is currently serving as the Chair of Budget and Finance Committee of the Faculty Senate at the University of Memphis.

Professor Rezaee has published over 230 articles and made more than 250 presentations, written 14 books and several book chapters and been invited as keynote speaker on business sustainability, corporate governance and Forensic accounting. Some of his books are : *Financial Institutions, Valuations, Mergers, and Acquisitions: The Fair Value Approach*; *Financial Statement Fraud: Prevention and Detection*; *U.S. Master Auditing Guide* 3rd edition; *Audit Committee Oversight Effectiveness Post-Sarbanes-Oxley Act*; *Corporate Governance Post-Sarbanes-Oxley: Regulations, Requirements, and Integrated Processes; Corporate Governance and Business Ethics and Financial Services Firms: Governance, regulations, Valuations, Mergers and Acquisitions. His sustainability related books are Corporate Sustainability: Integrating Performance and Reporting,* published in November 2012, won the 2013 Axiom Gold Award in the category of Business Ethics and *Business Sustainability: Performance, Compliance, Accountability, and Integrated Reporting* was published in October 2015 by Greenleaf Publishing. His most recent book on *Audit Committee Effectiveness* was published in in three volumes by Business Expert Press in July 2016. His "Corporate Governance aftermath of the 2007–2009 Global Financial Crisis" in four volumes and "Forensic Accounting" in two volumes are published by the Business Expert Press in July 2018 and March 2019 respectively. My book on "Business Sustainability, Corporate Governance and Organizational Ethics" is published by Wiley in November 2019. Several of these books are translated into other languages including Chinese, Persian, Korean, and Spanish.

Index

OTHER TITLES IN THE BUSINESS LAW AND CORPORATE RISK MANAGEMENT COLLECTION

John Wood, Econautics Sustainability Institute, Editor

- *A Book About Blockchain* by Rajat Rajbhandari
- *Successful Cybersecurity Professionals* by Steven Brown
- *Artificial Intelligence for Security* by Archie Addo, Muthu Shanmugam and Srini Centhala
- *Artificial Intelligence Design and Solution for Risk and Security* by Archie Addo, Muthu Shanmugam and Srini Centhala
- *Artificial Intelligence for Risk Management* by Archie Addo, Srini Centhala and Muthu Shammugam
- *The Business-Minded CISCO* by Bryan C. Kissinger
- *The Business of Cybersecurity* by Ashwini Sathnur
- *Equipment Leasing and Financing* by Richard M. Contino
- *Getting the Best Equipment Lease Deal* by Richard M. Contino
- *AI Concepts for Business Applications* by Nelson E. Brestoff
- *How New Risk Management Helps Leaders Master Uncertainty* by Robert B. Pojasek
- *Understanding Cyberrisks in IoT* by Carolina A. Adaros Boye
- *Cybersecurity Law* by Shimon Brathwaite
- *Conversations in Cyberspace* by Giulio D'Agostino

Announcing the Business Expert Press Digital Library

Concise e-books business students need for classroom and research

This book can also be purchased in an e-book collection by your library as

- a one-time purchase,
- that is owned forever,
- allows for simultaneous readers,
- has no restrictions on printing, and
- can be downloaded as PDFs from within the library community.

Our digital library collections are a great solution to beat the rising cost of textbooks. E-books can be loaded into their course management systems or onto students' e-book readers.
The **Business Expert Press** digital libraries are very affordable, with no obligation to buy in future years. For more information, please visit **www.businessexpertpress.com/librarians**. To set up a trial in the United States, please email **sales@businessexpertpress.com**.

www.ingramcontent.com/pod-product-compliance
Lightning Source LLC
Chambersburg PA
CBHW061334220326
41599CB00026B/5189